The Handbook
of Slogans

The Handbook of Slogans

Lionel Salem

The Handbook of Slogans

This first edition published in Great Britain 2012 by Crimson Publishing Ltd
Westminster House
Kew Road
Richmond
Surrey
TW9 2ND

© Crimson Publishing Ltd, 2012

The right of Lionel Salem to be identified as the author of this work has been asserted by him in accordance with the Copyright, Designs and Patents Act, 1988.

A catalogue record for this book is available from the British Library.

ISBN 978 1 78059 036 3

Typeset by IDSUK (DataConnection) Ltd
Printed and bound in the UK by TJ International Ltd, Padstow, Cornwall

DEDICATION

To Enid and Curtis

CONTENTS

INTRODUCTION

Why a handbook of slogans?

A good friend told me the word "slogan" apparently originates from the Scottish-Gaelic "sluagh-ghairm", meaning "war cry". Indeed I would define a company's slogan as a powerful phrase – the "cry" – which refers unmistakably to that company and its products, and to none other. This implies that hearing or seeing that phrase, whether on radio, TV or in the street, will automatically recall that specific company to the listener/viewer's mind.

We recognise advertising slogans as short phrases used by companies to emphasise the key aspects of a company's products or services. These are designed to be memorable phrases consumers will subsequently associate with the subject of the campaign and will ensure further and continued attention is drawn to the products or services. The word "memorable" implies the aforementioned recall. Whatever the case, anybody who even skims through the 2,500+ slogans of this book will soon have their own personal idea of what a slogan is and what it stands for.

From slogans which are older than most of us ("Never knowingly undersold", John Lewis, 1925; "A diamond is forever"**, De Beers, 1947; even "Because I'm worth it"*, L'Oréal, 1973) to slogans which will have soon come of age ("Begin your own tradition", Patek Philippe, 1996; "J'adore Dior"**, 1999) to very recent "infant" slogans which have yet to prove their worth ("Live in the now", *Wall Street Journal*; "Go forth", Levi's; "Take one small step", Barclays, all 2009–10), companies have come to realise the importance of slogans in their marketing strategy.

Hence the rush to create new slogans is on. Just take a look at Mercedes, Jaguar or Ford – companies which have produced nearly half a dozen slogans each in the past decade. Car companies, however, can be forgiven for producing multiple slogans because they often feel that each new model requires a slogan of its own. Other companies which never had a slogan now feel the urge to discover and brand an expression which will help remember what they do and why they exist: for example,

Heathrow's "Making every journey better" and British Gas's "Looking after your world" were both companies' first slogans and both coined in 2009.

As mentioned above, the main purpose of a slogan should be to impinge lastingly on the consumer's mind. Get them to dream! "A diamond is forever"** is so well-known it has inspired a household phrase (and a globally renowned music score for Shirley Bassey), without the person using it necessarily remembering its origin or the company it is associated with. The same applies to L'Oréal's "Because I'm worth it"*, apparently recognised by more than 70% of household women in the USA.

More specifically a high-quality slogan must be short, powerful and yet (herein lies the difficulty in generating an excellent slogan) say as much as possible about the company; whether it be its field or its products. In this manner, you unmistakably recognise that particular company, and none other. In this respect, "Intel Inside"** is a model slogan. First, it is short – only two words. Second, this repetition of similar-sounding words makes a powerful combination, sounding like a drum. Third, the word "inside", albeit not perfect, is probably one of the best single words one can think of to describe Intel's products. Finally, as the icing on the cake, the reiteration of two words starting with the same syllable ("In … in …") creates a glamorous slogan. Another excellent slogan which obeys these criteria is "Today. Tomorrow. Toyota"*. Although the third criterion is somewhat less well respected, "Today. Tomorrow." does possibly imply longevity but not necessarily a car product rather than say a washing machine or a TV set.

It is important to note that a short slogan is not necessarily an asset. Suppose De Beers had simply used the slogan "Forever". One could have immediately objected that this non-specific slogan was excellent for diamonds but also for long-lasting raincoats or laptop computers!

Finally, it's worth noting that some companies do not feel the need to have a slogan at all, presumably because they believe their product or service speaks for itself or that the company is sufficiently well-known for what they deem the "right" associations. One of these is Ferrari; although the company did allow the prancing horse logo and the beautiful "Beyond Perfection"** slogan to be used in ACER's Ferrari laptop advertisements. Google also has no slogan whatsoever – just a mission to make sense of the world's information and avoid doing "evil" – yet its employees show great imagination in presenting the word "Google" on the home page of their website with the most amusing 'eye-catches'. A lesser-known company in the same situation is confused.com. In the past few months this company has literally bombarded UK TV channels with adverts enticing people to get insurance quotes through their website (see "30 seconds to impact: how to make a confused.com TV ad" at www. confused.com for an interesting insight into the making of their TV adverts). Yet, something important is missing from these ads: a slogan! Maybe by the time this book is published the company will have found such a slogan.

How to use this book

Immediately following this introduction you will find my selection of two-star slogans (the top 1%) and one-star slogans (the next 6%). This is a deliberately short and purely personal selection of the most impactful and successful slogans in the book. There are many slogans without stars which I admire, and I have highlighted these in the main text, but the starred slogans are my choice of the very best. You will doubtless disagree with some of my selections and omissions, although I hope once you have read my comments in the main text you will understand them. If you would like to email me your thoughts you can do so at handbookofslogans@ crimsonpublishing.co.uk.

After that comes the main part of the book – some 2,500 notable slogans of one kind or another, mostly good examples of the craft but also some interesting failures. These are arranged alphabetically by main industry, and then alphabetically by company/brand name within each industry. For ease of use I have tried to use the most commonly-recognised company or brand name, which is not always the official name of the main company. While comprehensive, this list is not an exhaustive one (or the book would run to many thousands of pages!). I have not tried to include every single slogan a company has used, but the ones that appeared most frequently. Inevitably some new, interesting slogans will have appeared whilst the book was being produced. I haven't been able to include them here but do email me with any you think should be included in a future edition of this book.

The third part of the book tells the stories behind 61 of the best-known slogans. These are not necessarily the best slogans, but the most illuminating.

And then there are two indices for ease of reference, one by company name and one by theme.

Acknowledgements

I would like to thank Alison Hemmings and Daniel Salem and other friends who kindly suggested slogans I was unaware of, and also my tireless editor, Ian Wallis, and his colleagues at Crimson Publishing

Lionel Salem

TWO-STAR SLOGANS

The 25 slogans below are the author's top 1% of the featured slogans and are distinguished throughout the book by a double asterisk symbol (**). (For more details, see Introduction, p.xi.)

Beyond perfection (ACER)

The ultimate driving machine (BMW)

Beyond petroleum (BP)

A diamond is forever (De Beers)

We move the world (DHL)

J'adore Dior (Dior)

Better things for better living (DuPont)

Unmistakably (Graaff)

Live it. Love it! (Hong Kong)

Intel Inside (Intel)

Life's Good (LG)

Oh My Lord & Taylor (Lord & Taylor)

Where's *your* moustache? (Milk)

Morgan means more (JP Morgan)

Just do it (Nike)

Connecting people (Nokia)

Welcome back (Prozac)

Know Now (Reuters)

Our forecast is for more showers across the country (Ripples)

So easy to enjoy. So hard to forget (Singapore)

Be one (Starwood Preferred Guests)

And so to bed (Tempur)

The ultimate address (The World)

Where brands get their break (TV)

Consider it done (UPS)

ONE-STAR SLOGANS

The 150 slogans below are the author's next 6% of the featured slogans and are distinguished throughout the book by a single asterisk symbol (*). (For more details, see Introduction, p.xi.)

For all walks of life (Allen Edmonds)

Have a happy period. Always (Always)

Works like a dream (Ambien)

Think fast. Thing egg (American Egg Board)

What's your share? (Ameritrade)

Real mining. Real people. Real difference (Anglo American mining)

One element runs rings around them all (Anglo-gold)

So easy to use, no wonder it's #1 (AOL)

Think different (Apple)

Noah's route. Your route (Armenia)

Together (Bacardi)

You make it what it is (BBC)

The tougher the deal the more we enjoy it (Bingham)

Thinking beyond banking (BNP-Paribas)

A passion for perfection (Breitling)

Follow the herd (Buffalo's)

Born for ice (Bulmer's)

You can (Canon)

How many lives have you changed today? (CARE)

Carpets with soul (Carini Lang)

Probably the best beer in the world (Carlsberg)

What about Belgium? (Carlsberg)

Give more. Give Carte d'Or (Carte d'Or)

Now you're really flying (Cathay Pacific)

Sophisticated Food for Sophisticated Dogs (Cesar)

Just the right amount of wrong (Cosmopolitan Hotel, Las Vegas)

Let's talk (Crédit Lyonnais)

The difference is Crystal clear (Crystal Cruises)

Engineering with passion (Dassault Systèmes)

Life made fabulous (Debenhams)

Spray on. Play on. (Deep Freeze)

You can tell it's Dell (Dell)

Born to move (Delsey)

On top of the world (Delta Airlines)

Beautiful people (Dim)

The luxury of freedom (Dior)

Discover the difference (Dove)

The miracles of science (DuPont)

The architects of time (Ebel)

Miss nothing (ESPN)

Every second counts (ESQ)

Famous for a reason (The Famous Grouse)

Escape the ordinary (Finnair)

Unbeatable (Flight Centre)

Feel the difference (Ford)

Drive one (Ford)

Master of complications (Franck Muller)

Take care (Garnier)

A better way (Gateway)

Imagination at work (General Electric)

Today, time begins (Graaff)

Be a pioneer (Greenland)

Not long haul but miles away (Guernsey)

Guinness is good for you (Guinness)

Making heads happier (Head & Shoulders)

We listen, you hear (Hidden hearing)

Stay smart (Holiday Inn Express)

The power of dreams (Honda)

ENGINEUS (Hyundai)

Opportunity doesn't knock. It emails (Inquisit)

Nothing comes between you and the best price (Instinet)

We know what it takes (InterContinental Hotels)

Don't dream it. Drive it (Jaguar)

There's only one (Jeep)

Nothing similar is quite the same (Jim Lawrence)

Keep walking (Johnnie Walker)

The car that cares (Kia)

The bold look of Kohler (Kohler)

Helping people help themselves (Kuwait Fund)

My point of view (Leica)

For the journey... (Lloyds TSB)

Your home away from home (Mandala Hotel, Berlin)

Where nothing is overlooked except Hyde Park (Mandarin Oriental Hyde Park)

You can't predict. You can prepare (Mass Mutual)

There are some things money can't buy. For everything else there's MasterCard (MasterCard)

Simply divine (Mauritius)

Good to the last drop (Maxwell House)

Our doctors go to places photographers don't (Médecins sans Frontières)

The future of automobiles (Mercedes-Benz)

A tradition of trust (Merrill Lynch)

Human achievement (Merrill Lynch)

The best care in the air (Midwest Express Airlines)

Makes your tastebuds tingle (Mr Todiwala's)

Bull or bear, we don't care (Momentum AllWeather)

One client at a time (Morgan Stanley)

Nespresso, What else? (Nespresso)

Good food. Good life (Nestlé)

Save the Sound (Olive)

The future's bright, the future's Orange (Orange)

L'Oréal because I'm worth it (L'Oréal)

Even at sea level you can feel on top of the world (Oyster Yachts)

Great at Kleening (not so good at spelling) (OzKleen)

Peaceful nights. Playful days (Pampers)

History always leaves a trace (Panerai)

The fountain of youth for patio furnishings (Patio Magic)

Motion & emotion (Peugeot)

Go on. Give in (Pillsbury)

Because the unexpected happens (Plan B)

Just my style (Playtex)

Your pet, our passion (Purina)

Providing emotions since 1534 (Quebec)

Choose your own destiny (Radiance)

It's time for a Renaissance (Renaissance Hotels)

Distinctly above it all (Reynolds Mountain)

Bursting with bubbling Berryness (Ribena)

Perpetual spirit (Rolex)

Move your mind (Saab)

Making life taste better (Sainsbury's)

Need knows no season (Salvation Army)

It's dry. But you can drink it (Savanna)

Spend a third of your time in first class (Savoir Beds)

Keeping Britain on its feet (Scholl)

Escape to reality (Science Museum London)

Where else? (Sears)

Who owns who? (Seat Leon)

From sharp minds come Sharp products (Sharp)

Sharpens your thinking (Sheffield Hallam University)

The future is calling (Siedle Scope)

The soda Nature would drink *if* Nature drank soda (Sierra Mist)

Fuel the fun (Skippy peanut butter)

From www to zzz ... (Sleeproom. com)

Open your mind (Smart)

Be there (Smirnoff)

Discover the difference (Sofasofa)

Lost at last! (Spain)

Champagne for the brain (*The Spectator*)

History begins every morning (Tag Heuer)

Outsmart Mother Nature (Tampax)

Expect more. Pay less (Target Stores)

Wherever. Whenever (Tata Motors)

Exceed your expectations (Thailand)

Be part of the time (*The Times*)

Join the conversation (*Time*)

Innovators by tradition (Tissot)

Our energy is your energy (Total)

Today. Tomorrow. Toyota (Toyota)

Be there first (United Technologies)

Bringing light to life (Velux)

Be merry be bright be colourful (Vera Bradley)

Kiss your data hello (Veritas)

Rule the Air (Verizon Wireless)

Love at First Flight (Virgin Atlantic)

Das auto (in German: the car) (Volkswagen)

For life (Volvo)

Live in the know (*Wall Street Journal*)

Feel every word (Waterstone's)

Immerse yourself (Wildlife & Culture Holidays)

The real deal (Winn Dixie)

Where the past is always present (Yesterday)

PART 1
SLOGANS

AEROSPACE

Airbus Industrie
1) Travel in peace
Excellent; alleviates the fear of flying
2) Setting the standards

Boeing
1) Forever new frontiers
2) Can we give you a lift?
3) Together we fly higher
4) It's more than a dream
It's getting better, but it still lacks the killer punchline

Cessna (Textron)
1) With you for 70 years. Making history
2) Building futures

CMF
The power of flight

Cordant Technologies
When it better work, we make it work better

Dassault Systèmes
Engineering with passion*

EADS
The step beyond

Lockheed Martin
Mission Success begins with partnerships

Northrop Grumman
Defining the future

United Technologies
Be there first*
Little to say about this premium slogan, although it is not very specific

AIRLINES, AIRPORTS

Aer Lingus
Great Care. Great Fare
Nicely put in a nutshell

Air Canada
A breath of fresh air

Air France
Making the sky the best place on earth

Air India	Come fly with me *Was withdrawn because it was* *considered too sexist*
Air Namibia	Carrying the spirit of Namibia *A bit redundant*
Air New Zealand	We'll go to the ends of the earth for you *Rather than the slogan, it is the photo of the* *earth (seen as a half-moon) which is really* *splendid*
American Airlines	1) Something special in the air 2) We know why you fly
Asiana Airlines	The Jewel of Asia
Austrian Airlines	1) The most friendly airline 2) Fly with a smile
Biman (Bangladesh Airlines)	Your home in the air
Brit Air	The pioneering spirit
British Airways	1) The world's favourite airline 2) The way to fly 3) To fly. To serve
British Midland International	1) A small token of our love 2) Love that winter sun
Cathay Pacific	1) The heart of Asia 2) Now you're really flying* *This slogan has a lot of punch in it* 3) Great service. Great people. Great fares *A slogan in the form of a trilogy of* *two-word statements – we'll meet many* *in this book*
Cayman Airways	Those who know us love us

Continental Airlines   Work hard. Fly right

Delta Airlines   On top of the world*
Double meaning; passengers fly over the world, and as the saying goes, they feel great, "on top of the world"

Delta Skymiles   Your next vacation is closer than you think

EasyJet   1) Come on. Let's fly
Friendly slogan, but says nothing about the airline itself

2) Brilliant fare. Brilliantly fair
Progress, but a bit overweight

Emirates   1) The finest in the sky

2) Keep discovering
Quite strong – not far from deserving a star

3) A friend of Europe
A new direction in the company's advertising!

Etihad Airways   The world's leading airline

Finnair   1) Here for the evening

2) The fast airline between Europe and Asia
Too much insistence on speed

3) Escape the ordinary*
This time, bang on!

Flight Centre   Unbeatable*
It is interesting that such a good single word, which says a lot even though it is not specific, has not been used by any other company

Gulf Air   1) Redefining business travel

2) Come smile with us
Much better than the first slogan

Heathrow   Making every journey better

Hong Kong Airlines   Not business as usual

Iberia	1) Committed to move your world
	2) We've outdistanced the competition
	Too boastful
Japan Airlines	A better approach to business
KLM	Journeys of inspiration
Korean Air	Excellence in flight
Lot (Polish Airlines)	Perfection above all
Lufthansa	1) More than just flying
	2) There's no better way to fly
Malaysia Airlines	Going beyond expectations
Midwest Express Airlines	The best care in the air*
	Nice rhyme
Monarch Airlines	How low-cost airlines ought to be
NetJets	The only airline you'll want to buy shares in
Qantas	Enjoy the journey
Qatar Airways	1) Taking you more personally
	2) World's five-star airline
	Better because it's more to the point
Sabena	Enjoy our company
Singapore Airlines	A great way to fly
Sky Team	Caring more about you
Star Alliance	1) The airline network for Earth
	2) The way the Earth connects
Swiss [fusion of Swissair with Crossair]	1)The refreshing airline
	Used to be "The world's most refreshing airline". Better as it is
	2) Our sign is a promise

TAP	Fly higher
Thai Airways	Smooth as silk
Turkish Airlines	Globally yours *At first this slogan looks rather dull —* *but it has a lot of information.* *"Globally" means the airline spans* *the whole world; and "yours" means* *that it is client-friendly.*
United Airlines	1) Rising 2) We are United *Nice pun* 3) It's time to fly
Virgin Atlantic	1) Love at First Flight* *The replacement of "sight" with "flight"* *makes for an evocative slogan* *playing on the mutual attraction* *between customer and company* 2) *Je ne sais quoi.* Defined *The first part of the slogan* *intelligently utilises a familiar French* *expression* 3) Fear of not flying *Not very good, because it brings in the word* *"fear" often associated with flying* 4) Your airline's either got it or it hasn't

ANTIQUES, ART

Althorp	Living history *A good definition of an antique*
Anthony Woodburn	Fine antique clocks
Chelsea Trading Company	Serious art for the budding collector
Michael Sim	Fine English furniture
Solomon Bly	Continuing a tradition est. 1831

AUTOMOBILES, BICYCLES, MOTORCYCLES

AA (Automobile Association)	For the road ahead
Abarth (Fiat)	A world of empowerment
Acura (Honda)	1) The true definition of luxury. Yours 2) Style to command the road. Performance to own it
Alamo	Travel smart
Alfa Romeo	1) *Cuore sportivo* (in Italian: A sporting heat) 2) Beauty is not enough 3) Without heart we would be mere machines *Nice but a bit of a heavy contrarian statement; others would have written the less attractive "A machine with a heart"*
ASX	Intelligent motion
Audi	1) The world is our market 2) Open up your world
Aurora (GM)	Defy convention
Avis	We try harder *A very old slogan, dating back to when Avis said "We're no. 2 ... but we try harder"*
BMW	The ultimate driving machine** *Excellent association of the future (ultimate) and the past (driving machine)*
Bridgestone	1) Passion for Excellence 2) Your journey, our passion *The word "journey" now refers to the field to which the slogan is relevant*
Brooklands Museum	The vintage sports-car club

Brooks   Enjoy every mile

Brotherwood   The leading car scheme for disabled people
Slightly long-winded, but sometimes one has to spell out in detail the company's objective

Buick   Luxury. Pure and simple

Cadillac Coupé   The new standard of the world

Cadillac CTS   Break Through

Cadillac Eldorado   Live without limits

Carcraft   Drive happy

Cars (Classic Automotive Relocation Services)   Traditional values. Modern thinking

Chevrolet   1) Get real
2) It's a big plus

Chevrolet Cavalier   We'll be there

Chevrolet Tahoe, TrailBlazer   Like a rock

Chrysler   1) Cars from the heart
2) Drive = love
I find this slogan too facile
3) Luxury liberated

Citroën   1) Nothing moves you like a Citroën
In spite of the nice use of the double meaning of "moves", the earlier French version, without a negative, is better: "C'est fou tout ce que Citroën peut faire pour vous" (in French: It's incredible what Citröen can do for you)

2) Créative technologié
The slogan is in French – with an accent on the e of "créative" and "ie" at the end of "technologié" – but tries to have the best of both worlds by putting the two words in the order of the English language rather than the French!

Citroën CS4 Why conform?

Continental Tyres When braking counts

Daimler-Chrysler Answers for questions to come

Delphi Driving tomorrow's technology

DMS Automotive Unleashing Performance

Dodge Grab life by the horns
Refers to the Dodge logo of a ram

Dunlop Drivers know

Enterprise We'll pick you up

Farécla [scratch remover] World Class Surface Finishing

Ferrari 1) Passion
For the absence of any real slogan, see the article on Ferrari on page 165

2) Approved
This term is only specific to Ferrari used cars

Fiat Punto Open your eyes

Ford Motor 1) Travel first class
Not very good because of the obvious confusion with plane, or even train, travel

2) No boundaries
3) Feel the difference*
This slogan grows on you – and isn't far from deserving a second star

4) Drive one*
Unexpectedly good slogan!

Garmin Garmin, your guiding angel
Charming

GMC 1) You're due. Definitely due
2) We are professional grade

Golf Cabriolet The Golf amongst the cabriolets
Rather smart slogan, after you get the point

Goodrich	Fun is not a straight line *Intriguing; makes one think*
Halfords	That's helpful. That's Halfords.
Hertz	Love the road
Hilton & Moss	Achieving perfection
Honda	1) First man, then machine 2) The new pilot 3) The power of dreams* *The latest and by far the best*
Hummer	Like nothing else
Hyundai	1) Serving is believing 2) Win 3) Drive your way 4) New thinking / New possibilities 5) ENGINEUS* *What a beauty! Fantastically clever mix of the automobile "engine" and of the smart word "ingenious"*
Infiniti (Nissan)	1) Own one and you'll understand 2) Accelerating the future 3) Inspired performance
Isuzu	Go farther
Jaguar	1) Don't dream it. Drive it* *Very potent in spite of the negative in the first part; the three d's drive the point home, and there is a perfect mixture of dream and reality* 2) The art of performance 3) Born to perform
Jeep	1) There's only one* *A good way of singling out the uniqueness* 2) Only in a Jeep 3) The things we make, make us

11

Kia

1) The car that cares*
Neat alliteration; and "cares" has some phonic resemblance to "Kia"
2) Make every mile count
3) The power to surprise

**Land Rover
[see also Rover]**

Drive a hard bargain
The word "hard" is excellent here, because it alludes to the robust nature of the car

Lexus

1) The relentless pursuit of perfection
The word "relentless" really adds very little and lengthens the slogan unnecessarily
2) It's the feeling inside

Lincoln

1) American luxury
2) Reach higher

Maserati

1) The only car in its class
Smooth, but a bit too lengthy to deserve a star
2) Excellence through passion
This slogan has more gusto, but suffers from the fact that it could apply to any field

Maybach

Leadership is about seeking perfection

Mazda

1) Defy convention
2) Have it all

Mercedes-Benz

1) Unlike any other
2) Engineered like no other car in the world
This slogan, like the previous one, underlines the uniqueness of the brand
3) Once you drive one, there's no turning back
4) The future of automobiles*
Certainly the best of the lot, since it conveys the idea that the entire field depends on this brand
5) The best or nothing
Persuasive but we're getting away from cars

6) Welcome
The company follows the trend of shortening slogans

Mercury Imagine yourself in a Mercury

MG It's time to fall in love again

Michelin A better way forward

Mini Cooper Is it love?

Mini Cooper Countryman Expect big things

Mitsubishi
1) Built for living
2) Wake up and drive

Nissan
1) Driven
2) SHIFT_
3) SHIFT expectations
Better than no. 2

Nissan Micra In sync with the city

Oldsmobile Start something

Opel A sense of knowing

Peugeot
1) There are some things in life you never want to let go
Very wordy
2) Motion & emotion*
Great. Says it all in two words. Could have been two stars were it not for the "&" sign

Peugeot 207 The drive of your life

Pirelli Power is nothing without control
An unusual slogan, in a somewhat admonishing style

Pirelli Formula 1 Let's dance!

Plymouth Now that's imagination, that's Plymouth

Pontiac (GM)	1) Fuel for the soul
	2) Driving excitement
RAC (Royal Automobile Club)	The driving people
Range Rover	1) Designed for the extraordinary
	2) It's more than a new Range Rover. It's a new era
	3) Luxury, redefined
Range Rover Evoque	You don't have to shout to be heard
Range Rover Sport	Powered by intelligence
Renault	1) *Créateur d'automobiles*
	Easy to understand in English; like BMW, combines the old fashioned "automobiles" with the futuristic, "créateur"
	2) Drive the change
RM Auctions	Offering the world's finest motor cars
Rover	A class of its own
Saab	Move your mind*
	Great; thanks to the two "m"s
Saturn (GM)	1) A different kind of company. A different kind of car
	2) It's different in a Saturn
Seat Alhambra	Technology to enjoy
Seat Leon	Who owns who?*
	Nice; shows how infatuated you can become with your car
Skoda	Simply clever
Smart	Open your mind*
	Excellent; just slightly aggressive towards those who don't believe in the car
Subaru	1) The beauty of All-Wheel drive
	2) Uncommon sense

Suzuki

1) Ride the winds of change
2) Way of life!

Sync

Say the word

Tata Motors

Wherever. Whenever*
This slogan, rarely seen in Europe, does suggest that a car can go anywhere at any time

Toyota

1) Everyday
Clean single wording, but the word itself is a relatively weak one

2) One aim
Not much better, in spite of its simplicity

3) Today. Tomorrow. Toyota*
Persuasive, although the rhyme is not perfect

4) Get the feeling

5) Your Toyota is my Toyota
This slogan is more a guarantee pitch

6) Moving forward

Toyota Corolla

A car to be proud of

Toyota Yaris

The smart money's on Yaris

Triplewax

Wash & go

Vauxhall

A warranty that could last a lifetime

Vauxhall Meriva

Embrace life

Visteon (Ford)

See the possibilities

Volkswagen

1) Drivers wanted
Too far-fetched

2) Das auto (in German: the car)*
Somewhat boastful, but quite good – implies the ultimate car

Volvo

For life*
Brings in very nicely the idea of reliability and of eternal use

CHARITIES

Age UK   Improving later life

American Heart Association

It's the gift of a lifetime
The word "lifetime" is a bit heavy for a slogan

Breast Cancer Research Foundation

A cure in our lifetime
See previous slogan

Cancer Research UK   Where there's a will, there's a way

CARE

1) Where there's CARE, there's hope
2) How many lives have you changed today?*
Here the interrogative form, generally not successful in a slogan, provokes the reader

Enham [supporting disabled people]

Releasing potential

Global Fund   Born HIV Free

Habitat for Humanity   We're changing the world

International SOS   Worldwide reach/human touch

Kuwait Fund

Helping people help themselves*
A nice reiteration of the word "help"

Médecins du Monde

Nous soignons les blessures qui se voient et aussi celles qui ne se voient pas (in French: we cure the wounds which are visible and also those which are not)

Médecins sans Frontières

Our doctors go to places photographers don't*
Although I'm not quite sure this is the accepted slogan for the organisation, this caption on an empty page is remarkable

Multiple Sclerosis Society	Give with confidence
The National Lottery [UK]	Put Some Play in Your Day
National Trust [England, Northern Ireland, Wales]	Time well spent
NSPCC	Cruelty to children must stop FULL STOP
One	Do one good thing *The word "one" has a symbolic butterfly drawn above the "one"*
Oxfam	Be Humankind
St John Ambulance	The difference
Salvation Army	Need knows no season* *Nicely to the point*
Save the Children	No child born to die
Science Museum [London]	Escape to reality* *Lovely contrarian message – one expects a museum to be rather staid*
Skin Cancer Foundation	Go with your own glow
Smile Train	Changing The World One Smile at a Time
Stroke Association	Please remember us in your will
Transparency International	Fight corruption. It's your world
WaterAid	Thank you for being the change
World Food Programme (United Nations)	We feed the world
World Wildlife Fund	50 years of conservation

CHEMICALS

Aldrich Chemical Co   Chemists helping chemists in
                          research and industry

American Plastics   Make it possible
Council

BASF   Helping make products better

Bayer   Expertise with responsibility

Ciba   Value beyond chemistry
                          *This slogan tries to circumvent the
                          negative connotation of the word
                          "chemistry"*

Dow   Discovering chemistry on human
                          terms

DuPont   1) Better things for better living**
                          *In spite of the vague word "things", this slogan
                          is so famous it is impossible not to include it in
                          the top 25*
                          2) The miracles of science*
                          *The "o" in "of" is elliptic, like the oval around the
                          name "DuPont" ; almost as good as the former
                          slogan!*

Hoechst   1) Finding new ways
                          2) The future in life sciences

Huls   Discover the link to life

Sabic   The power to provide

CHILDREN

Bepanthen   1) As soft as ... a baby's bottom
                          2) Breathable nappy care ointment

Greatvine   Expert advice for life

Johnson's Baby Oil   A touch of magic

Pampers	1) Inspired by babies. Created by Pampers *In spite of its length, says a lot – puts babies in the driver's seat* 2) Peaceful nights. Playful days* *Lovely slogan. Repetition of the capital "P"s; and says everything in four words*
Stokke [prams]	1) Be together. Grow together 2) The only stroller you'll ever need 3) Always close to you

---

CLOTHING [SEE ALSO "RETAIL"]

7 Clothing	For all mankind
Abercrombie & Fitch	Casual luxury
Athleta	Get your run on
Austin Reed	For a change
Bali	1) Silver lining 2) Live beautifully
Banana Republic	1) Love the present 2) Life at work *Why this change?*
Belstaff	Since 1924
Brioni	To be one of a kind
Burberry	Touch *Pretty good; indeed one always touches clothes before buying*
C&A	Fashion and more
Citi	Live richly
Cotton Traders	Have you cottoned on yet?
Cotton USA	Naturally!

Debenhams	Life made fabulous* *Launched 31 August 2001. Excellent though non-specific*
DHB	Stay warm this winter
Diesel	1) For successful living 2) Be stupid *Another example of an a contrario slogan, where sexiness is promoted at the expense of intelligence*
Dim	Beautiful people* *Short and strong*
Dixies	Think summer – think Dixies
Donna Karan	Introducing the scent of luxury
Dressbarn.com	Live within your means. *Dress beyond them*
Dubarry	Where will you go in yours?
Eric Hill	Quality styles for discerning ladies
Ermenegildo Zegna	Passion for life
Falke	Falke or nothing
Fifty Plus	Fashion that fits your lifestyle
Figleaves.com	Everyday luxury for every body. *Note the separation between the two words "every" and "body". Women's bodies are the central theme of the ad*
Freddy	The art of movement
Freya Swim	Own the beach
GAP	For every generation
George [clothing at ASDA]	Excellent quality. Unbelievable low prices
Gore-Tex	Never stop exploring

Harvey Nichols	1) The world at your feet 2) Timeless clothes from you know Who *Compare with Schweppes*
Jones New York	Empowering your confidence
Joseph Abboud	Find your own element
Keds	The original sneaker
Lacoste	1) *Un peu d'air sur terre* (in French: some breathing space on earth) *Has a slightly ecological tone to it* 2) Unconventional chic *There is a slight redundancy in the meaning of these two words*
Land's End	Guaranteed. Period *Compare with Ameritrade*
Levi's	1) Have you ever had a bad time in Levi's? *Rather negative since opens up the possibility of criticism* 2) Go forth *In my opinion, far better*
L.K. Bennett	Life is the occasion
Lord & Taylor	Oh My Lord & Taylor** *Fantastic idea to put "Oh My" in front; this slogan will stick!*
Lou	*Emportez-vous, exaltez LOU* (in French: get fired up; glorify LOU)
Luckybrand.com	Live in your jeans
Marisota	Designed with you in mind
Marks and Spencer (M&S)	1) Quality worth every journey 2) Still turning heads *The TV ad which leads to this slogan is glorious* 3) Guaranteed second date
Merino.com	No finer feeling *Charming slogan*

Munsingwear	Munsingwear anywear *Pun on "anywhere"*
NYDJ [jeans]	Grab the spotlight
Pal Ziler	Quality without compromise
Piperlime.com	Let's get dressed
Playtex	Just my style* *A sporty slogan, which fits well with the idea of a contemporary, sporty woman*
Regatta	Great outdoors
S&K	America's men stores
Saks Fifth Avenue	Make it your own
Sears	Where else?* *In spite of the interrogative form, it's to the point*
Seraphine	Fashion for your pregnant curves *Elegant slogan in a difficult field*
Talbots	1) It's a classic 2) Tradition transformed *Note how this slogan goes a bit further than the previous one, by introducing the notion of change*
Timberland	1) Seek out 2) Go out and be you
Unno	Or not
Van Heusen	Shirts for men
Vera Bradley	Be merry be bright be colourful* *Well thought out*
Victoria's Secret	What is sexy?
WonderBra	An everyday WonderBra designed to put mother nature in her place
Woolmark	Take comfort in wool

Wrangler	1) Let Wrangler lead you from the straight and narrow 2) There's a bit of the West in all of us *See the progress, since now we pretty much know what Wrangler jeans are about*
Zilli	The finest garments for men in the world

COMMUNICATIONS [SEE ALSO "INTERNET, NETWORKS" AND "MEDIA"]

ADC	The broadband company
Agilent Technologies	Dreams made real
Alcatel	Broaden your life
Alltel	Always more than you thought
AMP	Connecting at a higher level
Astra	Your satellite connection to the world
AT&T	1) Your true choice 2) It's all within your reach 3) Networking 4) Rethink possible
AT&T [wireless]	Make your global life better
BellSouth	Listening. Answering
BlackBerry	Love what you do *Again, fastidiously, no reference whatsoever to the product*
Bouygues Telecom	*En faire plus pour vous* (in French: doing more for you)
British Telecom	1) Do business better 2) Bringing it all together

Cingular Wireless	What do you have to say?
CLS Communications	Your message matters
CoVad	Connect smarter
Ericsson	1) Make yourself heard
	2) Made for business. Good for life
	3) Taking you forward
	The third one is by far the best
France-Telecom	Let's build a smarter world
Galaxy (Samsung)	Where the possible begins
GTE	1) People moving ideas
	2) It's amazing what we can do together
Hicom (Siemens)	Communication unlimited
HTC	Quietly brilliant
Iridium	Calling planet Earth
Kinko's	Tap into the network
Kyocera	The new value frontier
Lucent	We make the things that make communications work
Lycamobile	Call the world for less
MCI World Com	1) Spoken here
	2) Easy to use worldwide
Micron Communications	Putting our stamp on automation
Nextel	Done
	The second shortest slogan after "Yes" from Lucozade
Nokia	Connecting people**
	Strong, only two words; yet includes both the technology and the clients

Northern Telecom (Nortel)	1) Communication networks for the world 2) How the world shares ideas 3) Business made simple
NTT DoCoMo	Beyond the mobile frontier
O2	We're better, connected *Note the importance of the comma in the slogan*
Orange	1) The future's bright, the future's Orange* *Like Société Générale, a play – and a nice one – on the colour* 2) The world is turning Orange
Orascom	1) Feel the world 2) Giving the world a voice
Qualcomm	The future of digital
Qwest	Ride the light
RadioShack	You've got questions, we've got answers
RM	Bringing learning to life
Siedle Scope	The future is calling* *Lovely use of words*
Skype	Take a deep breath
Sprint	1) The point of contact 2) The clear alternative to cellular 3) One Sprint. Many solutions 4) The Now Network
Station 12	The ultimate mobile connection
T-Mobile	1) Get more from life 2) Life's for sharing *Why the change? Because the company merged with Orange*

Talk Talk	A brighter home for everyone
Telcordia [formerly Bellcore]	Performance from experience
Verizon Wireless	1) We never stop working for you 2) Get it now! 3) Rule the Air* *Excellent, shows how progress can be made on searching for the appropriate slogan*
Vertu	Unparalleled communication
Vodafone	1) How are you? 2) Make the most of now 3) Power to you *The company doesn't seem to know the direction in which it wants to advertise itself*
Wanadoo	Positive generation

COMPUTING [SEE ALSO "INTERNET, NETWORKS" AND "SOFTWARE"]

ACER	Beyond perfection** *One could nearly say the same about this slogan, which seems so perfect. Compare with BP slogan*
APC	Legendary reliability
Apple	Think different* *An inspired way to emphasise originality, in only two words; however, the words are not specific enough to make one think of a computing company*
Asus	Inspiring innovation. Persistent perfection
Compaq	Inspiration technology

CompUSA	The computer superstore
Curry's PC World	We can help
Dell	1) Be direct
	2) Easy as DELL
	A take on "easy as Hell"
	3) The power to do more
	4) You can tell it's Dell*
	Fantastic because of the rhyme
Fujitsu-Siemens	We make sure
	Only superficially clever – it is really too vague
Gateway	A better way*
	Much better than the previous slogans "Connect with us" and "You've got a friend in the business". Great use of "way" in the slogan and in the brand name.
Hewlett-Packard	1) Invent
	Very short, but uses the imperative tense. Somewhat too close to the Intel slogan
	2) Everything is possible
	Identical to the Bang & Olufsen slogan. See also Adidas
	3) Everybody on
	The very latest one – not bad
IBM	1) Solutions for a small planet
	2) Deeper
	This pushes the trend to shorter slogans to the extreme; note the analogy with the super-computer "Deep-Blue" developed by IBM
	3) Smarter data for a smarter planet
Micron Electronics	1) Configured for your life
	2) Now you know
NEC	1) Imagination. Solutions
	Not good because it is trying to have the best of both worlds – and words. The two words are unconnected, so no clear message gets through
	2) Empowered by innovation
	Not much better

Olivetti	Computers worldwide
Palm	Business solutions
PlaceWhere	Log in. And meet
SanDisk	Move your world in ours
Seal & Vertu	Life. Beautifully arranged *The comparison with "life" is a bit far-fetched.* *Maybe "Alive" would have been more* *appropriate*
Siemens **[see also "*Enginnering*** ***and Materials",*** ***"Household" and*** ***"Internet, Networks"***	Global network of communications
Sun Microsystems	We're the dot in .com
Tandem	Reliability, no limits
Unisys	1) When information is everything 2) Imagine it. Done *Compare with UPS*
US Robotics **[see also 3 Com]**	1) The World's #1 Selling Modem *One of the few slogans, with E-Trade, to place* *the company's sales relative to the competition* 2) The intelligent choice in information access

CONSTRUCTION

Cemex	Building a better world
Cornforth	Considerate constructions
Eco	Recycled surfaces
FSB	It's in your hands
Italcementi	A world class local business

COSMETICS [SEE ALSO "HEALTHCARE" AND "PHARMACEUTICALS"]

Aussie [shampoo]

There's more to life than hair but it's a good place to start

Aveda

The art and science of pure flower and plant essences

Aveeno

Discover Nature's secret

Axe

The cleaner you are, the dirtier you can get
The word "can" is crucial here, because it explains that Axe not only cleans you, but allows you to enjoy yourself getting dirty afterwards

Bakel Oxyregen

Pure genius

Beyoncé [perfume]

Catch the fever

Bobbi Brown

Lasting looks

Britney Spears [perfume]

Choose your own destiny

Bumble and Bumble

Dedicated to the craft of hairdressing

Calvin Klein

1) For all for ever
2) What begins here never ends
The fundamental meaning is maintained from one slogan to the other

Calvin Klein Beauty [perfume]

It touches everything

Care New England

We touch your life like no one else

Chanel Chance [perfume]

It's your chance. Embrace it

Chanel Sublimage [skincare]

The infinite power of regeneration
Note that Chanel no 5 perfume has no slogan

Clairol Nice 'n Easy	Be a shade braver
Clairol Perfect10	Nice'n easy
Clarins	1) No one understands your skin better 2) Closer *to women* 3) Ultimate innovation
Clarins Eau des Jardins	Great fragrance, great feeling
Clear Express	The difference is clear
Clinique	Some things never change *A somewhat dubious stand for immobilism*
Clive Christian	The world's most expensive perfume *I am not sure this slogan will attract every client; and the company must prove that their ingredients are indeed as rare as they pretend*
Covergirl	Luxury touched by nature
Dior	1) The luxury of freedom* *Excellent. Instead of something like "the art of luxury", luxury comes in first and qualifies Dior at the outset; and the second word, "freedom", is essential for women* 2) *J'adore Dior*** (in French, but understandable in English) *For this lovely take-off of the brand name see also the article on Dior on page 157*
Dolce & Gabbana	The one
Dolce & Gabanna Sicily	Feel the passion
Donna Karan	Fragrances to seduce the senses
Dove	1) Difference clear to see *Again a pun on the clarity of our comprehension and the clarity of the soap residue* 2) Real women have curves *This advertising campaign celebrates real women; using larger models not the usual rather thin ones*

	3) Discover the difference*
	Far better than the others – only three words, and nice alliteration. Identical to Sofasofa's slogan
	4) Effective protection. Beautiful results
Dove Men + Care	Tough on sweat, not on skin
Dr Michael Prager	Look your best, naturally
Dr Sebagh Luminous Glow	Shining example
Elizabeth Arden Prevage	Proof . . . not promises
Estée Lauder	1) Defining beauty
	2) Every woman wears it her way
Garnier	Take care*
	Excellent: "take care" is often used at the end of a letter to say: "be in good health"; here this meaning is developed in a lovely way
Gillette Venus Spa Breeze [razor]	Reveal the Goddess in you
Givenchy L'Intense	The new fragrance
Got2b	Attitude for hair
Gucci Guilty [fragrance for men]	The new fragrance for him
Head & Shoulders	Making heads happier*
	This seemingly innocent slogan, for a product for which a telling slogan was not easy to find, is truly nice – treating the "head" as if it were a human being
Herbal Essences	It does beautiful things to your head
Hermès Voyage	Fragrance takes to the wing
Hugo Boss	Open minds. Free souls

Hugo Boss [eyewear]	Follow your vision
Insta-Dri	Beauty that works
Jergens	The beautiful difference *A rather pleasant slogan*
John Frieda Collection	1) The beauty of invention 2) It's a good day to dye *Slightly too daring*
Johnson's	1) Forever 2) For softness. For beauty. For life
Juvéderm	1) Ultra Smile 2) Siren Song
Kenzo	The world is beautiful
Kim Kardashian [perfume]	The voluptuous new fragrance
Lancôme	Believe in beauty *No comment here. Perfect slogan, even though not very specific*
Lancôme Teint Miracle	See the light
Lancôme Trésor	The fragrance for treasured moments *Note the discrete repetition of "trésor" and "treasured"*
Liz Earle	Naturally active fragrance
L'Oréal	1) L'Oréal because I'm worth it* *Note the use of the first person. I find this slogan rather exasperating, but apparently it works since the company keeps hammering it out; and the woman in the street has certainly heard about it, hence the star. (Note: in a new version "We're" or "You're" replace "I'm")* 2) *Professionnel* (in French: professional) *Less personal, but not bad* 3) *Recherche avancée* (again in French: advanced research) *The first time L'Oréal makes a bow to its famous research team*

L'Oreal Revitalift	It's not a facelift. It's Revitalift
Lubriderm	The skin therapist
Marc Jacobs	The fragrance for women
Max Factor	The make-up of make-up artists
Max Factor Makeover Collection	Transform yourself. Yourself *Dangerous but valid repetition*
Maybelline	Maybe she's born with it. Maybe it's Maybelline *Great rhyme. And great alliteration. Yet a bit too lengthy. This slogan is also accompanied by a song*
Murad	Transforming skincare
Neutrogena	1) Visibly firm 2) Beautiful. Beneficial
Nivea	1) Touch and be touched 2) Beauty is a statement 3) Feel closer 4) Pure and natural *Quite a lot of hesitation revealed by this succession of slogans – although the "purity" part seems right to the point*
Nivea For Men	Preparation is everything
Nubo	Accelerated recovery
Ojon	Nature's golden elixir
Olay	1) Challenge what's possible 2) Complete care
Olay Regenerist	Love the skin you're in
Old Spice	Smell like a man, man
Origins	Powered by Nature. Proven by Science
Palmer's Cocoa Butter Formula	Extraordinary results

Pantene	1) Don't hate me because I'm beautiful *This is apparently a very old slogan, mentioned to me by a friend, but which I have never seen in an advertisement* 2) The science behind healthy-looking hair 3) Healthy makes it happen *Nice alliteration*
Perry Ellis	The new fragrance for women
Physicians Formula Cashmere Wear [bronzer]	Your beauty. Our Passion. We Promise. *Same slogan as for Organic Wear*
Physicians Formula Organic Wear	Your beauty. Our passion. We promise *Same slogan as Cashmere Wear bronzer*
Pro-X	Potent. Proven. Professional
Purrs	Earn my affection *Too down-to-earth*
Radiance	Choose your own destiny* *Slogan sweeps through every domain, but still very forceful*
Ralph Lauren Romance	Always yours
Reveal	Reveal something . . . not everything
Revlon	Feel the love
Rimmel	Get the London look
Roc	We keep our promises
St Ives	Visibly healthy. Naturally Swiss
Sally Hansen	1) The science behind the beauty 2) Beauty that works
Sanex	Keeps skin healthy
Schwarzkopf	Professional Haircare for you

Secret [deodorant]	Because you're hot *Pretty daring, even for me!*
Silvikrin	The UK's most trusted hairspray
SK-II [facial treatment]	1) Touch the miracle 2) Live clear
Sonicare	A better kind of clean
Sure	It won't let you down
TRESemmé	Professional. Affordable
Vichy	Health is beautiful
VO5	1) Break the mould 2) *You* deserve to be treated as an individual *Clumsy*
Wella	Passionately professional *Good mix of the subjective and the objective*
White Diamonds	The fragrance dreams are made of *Although the perfume is associated with Elizabeth Taylor, I do not find this association of perfume/jewels to be very beneficial*
Witch Cosmetics	Naturally clear

EATERIES AND FOOD SERVICES [SEE ALSO "FOOD AND DRINK"]

Brakes	Fresh ideas *Cleverly implies the freshness of the food they supply*
Ffiona's	The best brunch in London
Hanks Seafood Restaurant [Charleston, SC]	Bring your Appetites *We have very few restaurants in this handbook, but there are a few deserving slogans*

Harvester	Salad & Grill
Micros	Helping your business to grow
Pizza Hut	1) Your favourites. Your Pizza Hut 2) Pizza and so much more
Ritter Courivaud Ltd	Importers and distributors of the finest foods
Starbucks.com	Natural fusions
Tchibo	Coffee Service
Woods Food Service	Delivering excellence

EDUCATION

ATM	The education union
Cass Business School	Cass means business *A good play on "meaning business"*
Hofstra University	We put learning on a pedestal
IMD	Real world. Real learning
London Business School	Transforming futures *"Your future" might have been better, since "futures" has two meanings*
Outward Bound	The adventure lasts a lifetime
Pennsylvania	Come invent the future
Rosetta Stone	Learn naturally. Speak confidently
Sheffield Hallam University	Sharpens your thinking* *Shows that a not too well-known university can create an excellent slogan*
Wharton	Executive education
Yale	Maybe you should be here too

ELECTRONICS

Alcatel-Lucent
1) The Hi-Speed company
2) At the speed of ideas

Best Buy
Turn on the fun

Hitachi
1) What's next?
Pretty good, were it not the interrogative form rather than the assertive form
2) Inspire the Next

Intel
1) Intel Inside★★
Superb; single word says where the Intel chip lies; two syllables in each; plus alliteration. If there were three stars available, it might get them!
2) Sponsors of tomorrow
I suppose even advertisers get tired of the best slogans. And "sponsor" is a weakish word

ITT Industries
Engineered for life

LG
1) Digitally yours
2) Life's Good★★
A good lesson on how to use meaningless initials for a great slogan. Makes good use of the abbreviation LG
3) We put people first

NEC/Mitsubishi
See more

Philips
1) Let's make things better
2) Sense and simplicity

Sanyo
Technology we can live with

SGS-Thomson Microelectronics
1) Isn't it time we met?
2) Bringing microelectronics to life
Uses too technical a word

Smith Corona
The way you want to work

Sony [see also "Entertainment"]
1) Go create
2) like.no.other
Interesting slogan, somewhat like an internet address

	3) make.believe *In my opinion the first one is the best, ie the oldest one*
Texas Instruments	1) Power to innovate the future *See Hoover* 2) Start doing extraordinary things
Thomson CSF	Securing your future
Toshiba	1) In touch with tomorrow *Nice alliteration* 2) Choose freedom
Voice Wing SM (Verizon)	It's how to call now

ENERGY

American Electric Power	America's Energy Partner *Note that the initials are the same*
America's Electric Utility Companies	The power to make life better
Areva	Energy experts
British Gas	1) Looking after your world 2) Energy smart *The two words are in different colours*
Conseco	Step up
Duracell	1) Trusted everywhere *Note that the "t" in the slogan is replaced by +, – to represent battery poles* 2) Rechargeable
EDF [France]	1) When your world lights up *I would have preferred "Light up your world!"* 2) Leading the energy change *Note how the slogan has adapted to ecological worries* 3) Save today. Save tomorrow *An extremely ecological slogan*
Energizer Max	For when you need it most

Enron	Natural gas. Electricity. Endless possibilities
eon	We're on it
General Electric	1) We bring good things to life 2) Imagination at work* *A really good one, which mixes dream with reality; really meant for the "health" side of GE*
Groupe Schneider	No one in the world does more with electricity
Kyocera	Doing what others dare not
National Grid	The power of action
Touchstone Energy	The power of human connections
Veba	The power to create value

ENGINEERING AND MATERIALS

ABB	Ingenuity at work
Arcelor	Steel solutions for man and earth
Artelia	Your success is our business
Black & Veatch	Expect success
Chiyoda	Engineering tomorrow's world
Dassault Systèmes [see also "Aerospace"]	See what you mean
Hydro	Progress of a different nature
JTA Connection	Makes it work
Lafarge	Materials for building our world *Too explicit. "Building our world" alone would have been better*

Siebe	Siebe the engineer. Here, there and everywhere
Siemens	Answers for mobility
Suez	Delivering the essentials of life
Timken	Worldwide leader in bearings and steel
Tyco	1) Unleashing the power within 2) A vital part of your world
uSwitch.com	uswitch.usave.usmile *Charming, and almost deserving a star*
Vinci	*Grands projets* (in French: important construction projects)

ENTERTAINMENT

Absolute Sounds	Set your music free
Aiwa	Power for pleasure
Arcam rCube	A listening revolution
Astra2Connect	The satellite broadband connection for everyone
Atlas Cables	Better by design!
Audio Emotion	Music is our passion
AVID HiFi	The truth, nothing more, nothing less . . .
Blockbuster	Don't forget you got it *Conveys the idea that you'll like the movie so much you won't give it back to your store*
Bose	Better sound through research
Cabasse	The legend goes on . . .
Cable & Wireless	What can we do for you?

DGM	Innovation that surprises. Technology that inspires *A bit clumsy*
Direct TV	Feel the joy
Electrocompaniet	If music *really* matters
Eton Corp	Reinventing Radio
Focal	The spirit of sound
Fort Myers-Sanibel	Welcome to island time
Guildford Audio	Run by professionals for professionals
Harman International	Hear us everywhere
Hitachi	1) A totally new vision *Note the double meaning of "vision"* 2) Inspire the next *Although this slogan has now been affixed on Hitachi buildings, it has a major flaw: "next" is not a noun, but an adjective – so it cannot be the complement to a verb . . .*
hmv	Get closer
IsoTek	The power to deliver "clean" power
Lehmann audio	High end by an audio engineer
Lovefilm.com	1) Find the films you want to watch 2) Love film, love life 3) Let's watch another one *The third is by far the better of the three slogans*
Mayflower Sounds	Hearing is believing
Motorola	Get ready *Rich in anticipation but could apply to any company*
MSNBC	America's news channel
Musicarch	Where beautiful Hi-Fi sings

NBC	More colourful
Olive	Save the Sound* *Very simple, with a good repeat of the "s" words*
Oxford Audio	We love to listen
Panasonic	1) Ideas for life *Nice aspect, but the relation to the company's field is not obvious* 2) Worldwide partner
Play.com	Free delivery of everything
Pro-Ject	Experience, gained . . .
Quad	The closest approach to the original sound
Regza	Image is everything
Samsung	Challenge the limits
Selectaudio	Exquisite audio products
Sevenoaks Sound & Vision	Real stories. Real people. Real products. Real value *A case of over-kill?*
Sharp/Aquos	There's more to see
Sony [see also "Electronics"]	Because you can
Trilogy Audio Systems	Designed & exclusively hand built in England
UPC	Say it your way
Vertere	Outperform
Virgin Media	A more exciting place to live
Vox Olympian & Elysian	Living voice
Zenith	1) Choose your own view 2) Digitise your experience

ENVIRONMENT

Bartlett [tree experts] For the life of your trees
Even if the original intention was not ecological, the slogan has an ecological resonance

Nature Conservancy Protecting nature. Preserving life

Oceana Protecting the world's oceans

Veolia The environment is an industrial challenge
Can be vastly improved

FAMILY

Ancestry.co.uk Who will you discover?

Findmypast.co.uk Search with the experts

FINANCIAL SERVICES [SEE ALSO "PERSONAL FINANCE"]

AIM Invest with discipline

All State 1) You're in good hands
2) The right hands make all the difference
Better, because the word "all" reappears

American Express 1) Do more
2) Realise the potential
I prefer the shorter one, although it could apply to many brands
3) Take charge
Possibly the best of the three, because it refers to the client's independence when travelling

Ameritrade	1) What's your share?*
	There's an interesting pun on the word "share"
	not used in the usual sense of a "stock", but in
	the "percentage" sense – accompanied by very
	funny ads
	2) The way to trade. Period
	Compare with Land's End
Bank One	Individual answers
Bearing Point (formerly KPMG Consulting)	Business and systems aligned. Business empowered
Bi-Lo	Everybody's favorite way to save
Brown & Co	I believe in the market. I believe in me
Capital One	1) What's in your wallet?
	Ambiguous; it's not clear whether the company
	wants to add to our wallet or . . . take from it
	2) Exclusive rewards. Enhanced security
Charles E. Schwab	The world's leading online broker
	Very close to E-Trade
Coopers & Lybrand LLP	Not just knowledge. Knowhow
CSA International	We answer with solutions
Cybertrade	There are traders. And there are cybertraders
Deloitte and Touche	The answer is . . . D&T
Deloitte Consulting	A very different approach. For very different results
Diner's Club	The right answer in any language
Donaldson, Lufkin & Jenrette	Putting our reputation online
	Nice play on the word "online"
Dow Jones	Be a better investor
Dreyfus Lion Account	Rule your kingdom

E-Trade	1) The #1 Place to Trade Online *Very close to Charles Schwab* 2) Someday, we'll all invest this way
Edward Jones	Invest in your dreams
Ernst and Young	From thought to finish *Pun on "from start to finish"*
EuroPages	Buy better, sell more
Everen Securities	A vested interest in your success
Farmers	Getting you where you belong
Fleet	Ready when you are
FM Logistics	Made with satisfaction
GE Capital Services	Our business is helping yours
Henderson Investors [UK]	Thoughts that count
Household	Helping everyday people. Everyday *Compare with Martha Stewart and MSN.8*
Instinet	Nothing comes between you and the best price* *Although somewhat immodest, this slogan is good because it conveys very clearly the advantages provided by the company*
Interactive Brokers	The professional's getaway to world markets
Jefferson Pilot	Investment. Insurance
JP Morgan	Morgan means more** *A nice use of the three "m"s and of the repeat of "mor"*
Jupiter	1) Leaders in long-term performance 2) On the planet to perform *Better and more to the point*
Kemper Funds	Long-term investing in a short-term world

Key Bank	Achieve anything
Lafayette Services (LaSer)	Customer value enhancer
Lincoln	Clear solutions in a complex world *The words "clear" and "complex" are not really complementary to each other*
Lombard Odier & Cie	Discretion in the art of asset management
McDonald Financial Services	Achieve anything
Mass Mutual	You can't predict. You can prepare* *Although unusually lengthy – six words – this slogan has good merit since a lot is said in those words*
MasterCard	1) There are some things money can't buy. For everything else there's MasterCard* *In spite of its great length, a slogan easily remembered* 2) The Future of Money 3) Priceless
Mellon Financial [see also BNY Mellon]	The difference is measurable
Merrill Lynch	1) A tradition of trust* *The repetition of "tr" adds to the strength of the slogan* 2) Human achievement* *A subtle mix of humanism and purpose*
Momentum AllWeather	Bull or bear, we don't care* *Good rhyme, good rhythm – says it all*
Montgomery Funds	Invest wisely
Morgan Stanley Witter	Measuring success one investor at a time
Neptune Income Fund	Invest in depth

Northwestern Mutual	Financial network
Norwich Union	No one protects more
NYSE	The world puts its stock in us
Oppenheimer Funds	The right way to invest
Pricewaterhouse Coopers	Join us. Together we can change the world
Prudential Financial	Growing and protecting your wealth
Salomon Smith Barney	1) Because we can, you can 2) Success is earned 3) They make money the old-fashioned way. They earn it
SAS Solution	The business of better decision making
Scottrade	We're all about value
ShiftPoint	Create/transform/deliver
State Street	For everything you invest in
Suretrader.com	The smart tool for smart investors
T. Rowe Price	Invest with confidence
TD Waterhouse	You're in control
TIAA-CREF	Ensuring the future for those who shape it
Transamerica	The people in the pyramid are working for you
Vanguard Group	Invest in our way of investing
Visa	1) The world's best way to travel 2) It's everywhere you want to be 3) It knows no boundaries 4) It's fluent in every language

	5) A bridge between the continents
	6) More people *go* with Visa
	7) Life flows better with Visa
	Slogans 3 to 5 don't really give an inkling about what the company does
Wachovia Securities	Uncommon wisdom
Washington Mutual	The Power of Yes
Winterthur	The experts in total risk management
Wonga.com	1) Little loans, lot of control
	2) Straight talking money
Zenger Miller	A reputation for results
Zenith Bank [Nigeria]	In your best interest

FOOD AND DRINK [SEE ALSO "EATERIES AND FOOD SERVICES"]

Absolut	1) Enjoy our quality responsibly
	2) Absolut envy
	Well constructed
	3) It all starts with an Absolut Blank
Actimel	Bring it on
ADM	Supermarket to the world
Altoids Smalls	Curiously strong. Curiously small
American Egg Board	Think fast. Think egg*
	Really strong; one readily associates the food "egg" with the positive adjective "fast"
Anchor [cream]	Every dessert deserves a squirt
Aptamil	Follow-on milk
Archers	Come out to play
Arctic Frutta	Break the ice

Arla   Closer to nature

Atkins   Feel the Atkins change

Auntie Val's   and nothing else
                     Emphasises that there are no artificial flavours

Bacardi   1) Drinks with attitude
                     2) Ready to serve
                     3) Together*
                     Quite nice – one of the best single-word slogans

Baileys   1) Let your senses guide you
                     Compare with Pier Import
                     2) Listen to your lips*
                     A daring union of "listen" and "lips", supposed to be smacking, or just pressing together
                     3) Let's do this again

Barilla   1) Taste that defies expectations
                     2) The choice of Italy
                     A wee bit nationalistic

Bass Ale   In a world of strange tastes, there's always Bass Ale

Beck's   Just part of the story

Beefeater Gin   Live a little

Béghin Say   *Un peu de sucre, beaucoup d'idées*
                     (in French: a little bit of sugar, a lot of ideas)
                     Note the careful "a little bit"! Sugar has become unpopular with dieticians

Benecol   Proven to lower cholesterol

Bertoli [sauces] Passion makes perfect

Betty Crocker   1) You and Betty Crocker can bake someone happy
                     The slogan is a bit lengthy but uses a great play on "bake" versus "make"
                     2) Expertise from our kitchen and yours

Bird's Eye Peas	We're only content with 100%

Blacksticks	A taste of the unexpected

Blue Dragon

The East made easy
Although the slogan doesn't refer explicitly to food, the word "easy" does touch on the asset of the company's food

Bombardier Beer

Bang on!

Bombay Sapphire [gin]

1) Pour something priceless
2) The spirit of exploration
3) Inspired

Bonne Maman

Moments to cherish
As a daily consumer of Bonne Maman jams, I feel that this slogan does not do justice to the brand, nor does it make use of the "Maman" in the brand name. Why not something like "Our mothers liked it. We love it. Our children adore it"?

Booker [food wholesaler]   Better service at Booker

Bordeaux

1) Fine wines. Be seduced
2) Good food would choose Bordeaux

Boursin

Du pain, du vin, du Boursin
It is quite extraordinary to see an ad for this company in a British weekly in French!

Brancott Estate [wine]

Stay curious

Brodies

The essence of quality

Budweiser

1) King of beers
2) True
3) Don't let the bubbles get in your way [Bud 66]
4) It's what we do

Buffalo's

Follow the herd*
Innovative; uses the company name in a smart way to find a strong slogan

Bulmer's

Born for ice*
Clever because evokes the drink itself only indirectly – yet gives an impression of freshness

Burger King

It just tastes better

Butler's

Welcome to the family

Buxton

A drop of pure Britain

Cadbury

Your happiness loves Cadbury

Cadbury Dairy Milk

A glass and a half full of joy
Slightly misleading – one might think the slogan refers to a drink, such as Cadbury Chocolate – even though the visual ads do show the glass of milk being used to make chocolate bar

Campbell's Chunky

It fills you up right

Carling

Brilliantly refreshing

Carlsberg

1) Probably the best beer in the world*
An interesting slogan, in that it boasts, but not too much – and it lets the reader make their final conclusion on the product. Note: in Copenhagen, on the central square, the slogan becomes "Probably the best beer in town"! In the UK the slogan is often used with the word "lager" instead of "beer"

2) What about Belgium?*
Although this is not a slogan proper, its repeated use in World Cup ads – "England 1, USA 1", "But what about Belgium?" – should have made it world famous. The actual slogan which follows is "Great taste, every sip of the way"

Carte d'Or

1) Give more, give Carte d'Or*
For once a French company has made an excellent effort to use a purely English slogan with an excellent English rhyme; however "Offrez plus, offrez Carte d'Or" was very good too

2) The final touch

Cassegrain

Cassegrain, une autre idée du légume (in French: Cassegrain, a different concept of vegetables)

Celtic Marches	Let the miracle begin
Chandon	Drink it in
Chivas	Live with chivalry *Good repetition of "chi" prefix*
Choc Chic	Guilt free chocolate *The brand name has a heart in the centre of the* *"o" of "choc"*
Clipper [tea]	Natural, fair & delicious
Clos du Bois [wines]	Rich as life
Co-operative	Good with food
Coca-Cola	1) The pause that refreshes *One of the first Coca-Cola slogans; dates back* *to 1929; still active* 2) Always *From 1993 to 2000* 3) The Coca-Cola side of life 4) Open happiness
Cointreau	The longest drink in the world
Colman's	Season & shake
Coors Light	1) Rock on *Pun with having a drink "on the rocks"* 2) The world's most refreshing beer
Copella	The fruit of our knowledge
Corona	Experience the extraordinary
Costcutter	Proud to be local
Courvoisier	Anything is possible in the state of Courvoisier
Cow & Gate [baby food]	Because healthy babies are happy babies
Coyopa	The world's best tasting rum
Curiously Cinnamon	Crave those crazy squares

Delverde	The true nature of pasta
Diet Chef	Enjoy losing weight
Diet Coke	Love it light
Disaronno	1) Taste the seduction 2) Open the possibilities
Dodgers [biscuits]	Get stuck in
Dolmio	When's your Dolmio day?
Domino's Pizza	It's what we do
Douwe Egberts	Your choice
Dove [chocolate]	Your moment. Your DOVE
Dr Pepper	What's the worst that could happen? *Dangerous slogan – question mark – and one* *wonders whether "Nothing better can happen",* *if available, might not have been better*
Drambuie	There are after-dinner drinks. And there's Drambuie
Dunkin Donuts	Just the thing
Eclipse	Beyond breath
Egg Marketing Board	Go to work on an egg *Very old 1950s slogan from the British Egg* *Marketing Board*
Estrella Damm	The beer of Barcelona
Evan Williams [whiskey]	Aged longer to taste smoother
Evian	1) From the French Alps 2) Live young *Far better*
Extra [chewing gum]	Worth chewing over
The Famous Grouse [whiskey]	Famous for a reason* *Nicely enigmatic*

FIJI Water	Untouched
Filippo Berio	The World's Finest Olive Oil
Foster's [beer]	Good call
French Bubbles [champagne]	Let's bubble
Galaxy [chocolate]	Think hiding it. Think Galaxy
Galaxy Ripple [chocolate]	Let the day unfold
Gatorade	Fuel that goes beyond hydration *The words "hydration" and "fuel" don't fit well together*
The Glenlivet Single Malt	1) Once discovered, always treasured 2) The single malt that started it all
Gordon's [gin]	Shall we get started? *A rare case where the question mark adds something to the slogan*
Gourmet Classic Cooking wines	Enhances your menu, increases your margin *A rare reference to profitability, a hush-hush word in slogans*
Gower Cottage Brownies	Bite me! *Excellent – the slogan makes the product talk*
Green Giant	Makes Mums Feel 10 Foot Tall
Grey Goose [vodka]	1) Sip responsibly 2) World's best tasting vodka *This one, at least, is as direct as can be* 3) To living in good company
Guinness	1) Guinness is good for you* *A famous slogan in Great Britain* 2) Bring it to life 3) Why let good times go bad? *Has the usual weakness associated with the interrogative form*

Gzhelka [Russian vodka]   Take me!
Same style, but not as good since there is no reference to the type of product

Häagen-Dazs   *Voyage pour vos sens* (in French: a journey for your senses)

Half Spoon (Silver Spoon)   All the taste but half the sugar

happy egg co.   Happy hens lay tasty eggs

Harveys Bristol Cream   Put your world on ice
A real crossword-like motto

Healthy Choice   Feel good food

Heineken   1) Heineken reaches the parts other beers cannot reach
2) Open your world
From a very specific slogan to a highly non-specific one

Heinz   1) No one grows ketchup like Heinz
Although the slogan limits itself to the world of ketchups, it's smart in situating itself at the top

2) Beanz meanz Heinz
3) It has to be Heinz

Hellmann's   Bring out the best

Hildon   Part of your life

Honey Dew (Fuller's)   Like lager? Love Honey Dew.

Horlicks   Made for evenings

Hovis   As good today as it's always been

Iceland   1) Food you can trust
Highly dangerous slogan – relative to the competition, which could feel insulted, and relative to themselves, if some day a slip up occurred
2) That's why mums go to Iceland

Innocent [orange juice]   Juicy by nature

Interprofesional del Aceite de Oliva Español [Spanish olive oil]	Everything's better with olive oil. Even you.
J20	Smile, tastebuds! *Charming*
Jack Daniel's	1) Not subject to change. Not now. Not ever 2) A singular experience
Jacques [cider]	Naturally styled
Jameson Irish Whiskey	1) Not just Irish 2) Easygoing Irish *These two slogans are somewhat contradictory*
Johnnie Walker	1) Keep walking* *Amusing reference to the man pictured on the label, and possibly a vague reference to Nancy Sinatra's "boots are made for walking"* 2) Our blend cannot be beat
Kashi	The seven whole grain company
Kellogg's Corn Flakes	The sunshine breakfast
Kellogg's Rice Krispies	1) Wonderfully simple 2) A recipe for fun
Kellogg's Special K	1) Get more delicious every day 2) *"Aimez-vous"* (in French: love yourself) *Great slogan in France*
Kenco	Believe in the taste
Kenco Millicano	Each millicule is special *A great invention of the word "millicule" – a take on molecule*
KFC	1) Finger-Lickin' Good 2) So good
KFC Krushems	Full of real Bitz

Kit Kat

1) Have a break. Have a KitKat
2) Make the most of your break

Knob Creek

Drink smart

Knorr

Dedicated to flavour

Kronenburg 1664

Slow the pace

**La Grande Dame
[champagne]**

For those who know

Lavazza

1) Espress yourself
2) *A modo mio* (in Italian: my way)

Lavazza Blue

Made for each other

Laverstoke Park Farm

When only the best will do . . .

Leerdammer

Not as mild as you might think

Lindt

Master Chocolatier since 1845

**Louis Roederer
[champagne]**

1) *De l'exception la règle* (in
French: We make a rule of being
exceptional)
2) Without compromise

Lucozade

1) Replaces lost energy
2) Yes
*Certainly the shortest of all slogans – but again
interchangeable to any company*

Lurpak

Good food deserves Lurpak
Why not "a better butter"?

M&M's

Melts in your mouth, not in your
hands
*Considered one of the most influential US
slogans in a 2007 survey. Yet, I buy the sweets
daily and had, till now, never heard of the
slogan . . . But my editor kindly points out that
this same slogan was used in the UK for
Minstrels in the 80s*

McDonald's

I'm lovin' it

McVitie's	Passion for cooking (*also*: "Passion for baking")
Magners	1) There's method in the Magners *Possibly inspired by Shakespeare's famous "Method in the Madness"* 2) Premium Irish cider
Magnum	1) The ultimate pleasure 2) For pleasure seekers
Magnum Mini	Do not disturb *Smooth, tempting*
Maille	Passion for food since 1747 *For similar types of slogans, see "Jewellery and Watches", "Sailing", etc*
Maltesers	The lighter way to enjoy chocolate
Mars	Work Rest Play *Does this slogan evoke a Mars bar to you?*
Martha Stewart	Everyday *Compare with Household and MSN.8*
Martini	*Veramente italiano* (in Italian: truly Italian)
Maxwell House [coffee]	Good to the last drop* *Really tasty; you feel you're drinking it*
Mentos	Save your mouth for Mentos
Mikado	You just can't help yourself
Milk	1) Where's *your* moustache?** *Very nice because it appeals to childhood memories at the breakfast table* 2) Got milk?
Milky Way	Bet you can't tell it's a lite
MonaVie [fruit juice]	Drink it. Feel it. Share it. *See Whole Foods for another example of this type of slogan*
Mountain Dew	Do the Dew

Mr Todiwala's [pickles]   Makes your tastebuds tingle*
A lovely slogan for a youthful company; would suggest that one of the more well-known food companies take it up

Napolina   The heart of Italian cooking

Nespresso   1) Coffee, body and soul
A play on the word "body", since one speaks of a wine's "body"

2) Nespresso. What else?*
Made famous by the TV ad with George Clooney

Nestlé   1) Sweet dreams you can't resist
Nestlé should be able to do better

2) Good food. Good life*
Nestlé must have heard my first remark, since this slogan is very good through its simplicity and the message it conveys

New York Bakery Co   The way bagels should be

Nutella   Wake up to Nutella
The ad pronounces "Nutella" in English, and the slogan was clearly a starter before the brand was introduced to the UK

Oasis   1) *Oasis, de l'eau, des fruits, du FUN*
(in French: Oasis, water, fruits, and FUN)
2) It'll go with anything
Neatly congenial, and far better than the previous one

Ocean Spray   1) Helps protect you inside
2) Good taste. From a good place
Far better

Old El Paso   Share the fun

"On" café [Asian food]   Home is where the heart is
This slogan, excellent per se, needs improvement when relating to the company

Patrón Tequila   Simply perfect
Compare with Wedding Paper

Pepperidge Farm   Never have an ordinary day

Pepsi Blue	It's a blue thing
Pepsi-Cola	1) Pepsi-Cola hits the spot 2) The choice of a new generation
Perle de lait (Yoplait) [yoghurt]	Pleasure makes you beautiful
Petits Filous	Be ready out there! *Somewhat "soft" slogan in spite of the ad showing "tough" kids. Indeed the French word "filou" means "a young rascal"*
PG Tips	Put the kettle on
Pillsbury	Go on. Give in* *Lovely, short, with good alliteration – and says what it has to*
Pimm's	1) Pimm's O'clock 2) Anyone for Pimm's?
Piper-Heidsieck	1) Red is not the colour of innocence 2) *Rien qu'une larme* (in French: literally just a tear, ie just a drop)
Poland Spring	Born better
Premier's Tea	Passion of purity
Président	*Bien manger, c'est le début du bonheur* (in French: eating well is the beginning of happiness)
Pringles	Celebrate with Pringoooals
Private Reserve Fries	Premium selected
Progresso	It's time to go Progresso
Quorn	Make one change. Make it Quorn
Rachel's	Find your Rachel's moment
Red Bull	Red Bull gives you wiiings *An interesting case where the word is modified to indicate the energy given by the drink. It's interesting to hear how it's pronounced in a TV ad*

Relentless Energy Drink   No half measures

Ribena   Bursting with bubbling Berryness*
A beautiful alliteration

Richmond [sausages]   It's the taste that brings them home

Ricola   Nature in its truest form

Ritz Crackers   Ritz it up!

Robinsons   A lot from a drop

Rougié foie [gras]   Can't be beaten on price or quality

Russian Standard   Vodka as it should be

Rutherford Hill   The taste takes you there

Ruth's Chris Steak House   It's the sizzle heard round the world

Ryvita   For ladies that crunch
This is a take on the expression "ladies who lunch"

Sainsbury's   Making life taste better*
Good mixture of sensory impressions – "taste better" – and of general living

San Miguel   It's not a quick beer

Savanna   It's dry. But you can drink it*
Lovely pun

Schweppes   Sch... you know who
*Compare with Harvey Nichols
Schweppes also ran a Nicole Kidman TV ad where she flees from a man's embrace to drink a Schweppes. "Hey what did you expect?" asks the actress*

Sheraton Tea   While there is tea there is hope!
I wonder if I wouldn't have replaced the "while" by "where" . . .

Shredded Wheat   Discover how good it can be

Sierra Mist   The soda Nature would drink *if* Nature drank Soda*
Lengthy but makes its point very well

Skippy [peanut butter]	Fuel the fun* *Great alliteration*
SMA Nutrition	Small steps, for their future
Smirnoff	1) Pure perfection 2) The greatest name in Vodka 3) Be there* *Smooth, although it's too non-specific – and not as boastful as the first slogan*
Splenda	Low calorie sugar alternative
Sprite	Obey your thirst
Stella Artois	1) She is a thing of beauty 2) Smooth lager 3) Reassuringly expensive 4) With a smooth outcome
Stolichnaya	Freedom of Vodka
Strongbow	Hard earned
Subway	Eat fresh
Tabasco	Release the flavour with Tabasco
Taco Bell	Think outside the bun
Taittinger	Dare to enjoy
Tesco	Every little helps
Tetley	That's better. That's Tetley
Tickler	Cheddar so precious you won't want to waste a crumb
Toblerone	Don't you wish all triangles were made of Toblerone? *The interrogative form is always dangerous but this slogan gets away with it*
Total [yogurt]	The yummy side of life
Trebor	Sweet success

Tropicana	Great tasting juice doesn't just grow on trees *Tries to convey the difficulty in making Tropicana juice, but somewhat clumsy*
TRS	Asia's finest foods
Truvia	Honestly sweet
Turning Leaf [wine]	Handcrafted to the smallest detail
Twinings	Gets you back to you
Twix	Two great tasting bars. Happy together *Right to the point*
Typhoo Tea	You only get an OO with Typhoo
Ultimat [vodka]	Live ultimately *This slogan shows a slight lack of imagination*
Uncle Ben's	1) Perfect every time 2) Great taste, nothing else
Unilever Food Solutions	Inspiration every day
Vimto	Seriously mixed-up fruit
Volvic	Filled with volcanicity *Nice invention of the slogan's word "volcanicity". An alternative is "Taste the fruity volcanicity"*
Walker's Crinkles	Fall in love with the groove
Walker's Extra Crunchy	Made for sharing – sometimes!
Wall's [ice cream]	Love ice cream
Wall's Sausages	What we want *Amongst the slogans with three words starting with the same letter, the very best*
Weber	Barbecues for life
Weetabix	Fuel for big days

Wendy's	You know when it's real
Wheaties	Breakfast of champions
Whole Foods Market	Whole people. Whole planet. Whole foods *For this popular "triple" appeal, see Monavie, Tipi and others*
William Lawson's	No rules. Great Scotch
Wiltshire Farm Foods	Delicious meals to your door
WKD	Have you got a WKD side? *Apparently "WKD" is often pronounced "wicked"*
Yakult	Listen to your gut
Zephyrhills [water]	Born better

FOOTWEAR

Adidas	1) Forever sport 2) Impossible is nothing *As pointed out to me by my editor, this goes further than the seemingly equivalent slogan "everything is possible" by Hewlett-Packard and Bang & Olufsen*
Allen Edmonds	For all walks of life* *Like Delta, a double-edged, incontrovertible motto*
Bass	Easy, American style
Blue Velvet Shoes	Clothes for feet
Caprice	Walking on air *And the butterfly logo nicely completes the ethereal impression*
Clarks	1) Feel the moment 2) Stand tall. Walk *More to the point*

Cole Haan	Stand for something
Emu	Naturally Australian
Etnies Jameson 2 Eco	Buy a shoe/plant a tree *An eco-friendly slogan*
FitFlop	1) Relief you can wear on your feet 2) Get a workout while you walk
Franco Sarto	The artist's collection
Havaianas	Always summer
Johnston & Murphy	The Best Shoes Anybody Can Buy *This slogan dates back to 1845; there have been* *variants with "money" replacing "Anybody"*
K-Swiss	Put your spin on it
Kenneth Cole	1) Reflect on what you stand for 2) Stand for something or step aside 3) Make a statement *Nothing left concerning shoes . . .*
MBT	Love the way they make you feel
Nike	1) I can 2) Just do it** *Again justifiably famous, as a song and as a* *slogan*
Primigi	An extraordinary adventure
Reebok	1) I am what I am 2) Run easy 3) Your move
Rockport	1) be comfortable. uncompromise. start with your feet *Note the absence of capital letters* 2) walkability
Scholl	1) All our design, all your style 2) Keeping Britain on its feet* *This slogan can be adapted to any country*

	3) great feet feeling
	4) Walk away from pain
Tod's	An Italian moment
Websters	A wider choice in footwear since 1964 *Tells us what the company does, but a bit clumsy*

FURNITURE [SEE ALSO "HOUSEHOLD"]

Ashville Inc	Luxury Builds, Refurbishments & Interiors
Bensons for Beds	Sound advice. Sounder sleep
BoConcept	urban design
Capitol Carpets	Carpets by Capitol . . . enough said
Carl Hansen & Son	Every piece comes with a story
The Carpet Foundation	Quality you can trust
Carpetright	We love floors
Clive Christian	Furniture for Luxury Homes of the World
Conquest	Fine bespoke furniture
Corona Lighting	It only gets better
Damac	Live the luxury
DFS	Think sofas, think DFS
Dreams	For a great night's sleep
Drexel Heritage	Welcome home
Furniture Village	You're in safe hands

goCreate [sofas]   mix it, match it, love it

Hammonds   Be inspired
See also Mark Wilkinson

Harveys   Bringing your home to life

Hayburn & Co.   For the finest homes

HSL   ... the chair specialists

IKEA   1) Make room for ideas
2) The life improvement store

Indian Ocean   Inspirational outdoor furniture

Jensen [beds]   Designed for sleep comfort

Jim Lawrence   Nothing similar is quite the same*
Excellent; nice play between the words "similar" and "same"

Lema   Not all houses are created equal

Ligne Roset   Beautiful statements

Limited Edition   Fashion for floors

Mark Alexander   Naturally beautiful fabrics

Mark Wilkinson   1) The finest furniture of our time
2) Be inspired
There is definitely a problem with this slogan: it is the same as Hammonds', and there is possibly an agreement for the mutual use of it. But what about Siemens?

Multiyork   Master furniture makers

Natuzzi   It's how you live

Neville Johnson   Design without compromise

The Odd Chair Company   Beyond the expected

Omoté   *Un état d'esprit* (in French: a frame of mind)

Plumbs ReUpholstery   Making your furniture beautiful again

Poltrona Frau   Cleverness/Intelligence in our hands

Roche Bobois   1) Your senses have a memory
2) 50 years of creation

Savoir Beds   Spend a third of your time in first class*
Lovely, albeit lengthy. Previously the slogan was simply "Since 1905"

Sharps   Space you never thought you had

The Sleeproom.com   From www to zzz . . .*
Smart slogan. The www implies the internet search; the zzz the falling asleep

Sofa.com   Caution! may cause drowsiness
A slogan with a sense of humour

Sofas & Stuff   experts in comfort

Sofasofa   Discover the difference*
*Rather good; would have become well-known if the company were larger
Identical to Dove's third slogan*

Sweetpea & Willow   Divine French furniture

Thomas Lloyd   Makers of fine furniture for generations

Thomasville   So you
Too impersonal; could be used in any field

Vi-Spring   Life changing

GAMBLING

PartyPoker.com	The world's largest poker room
Pinnacle Sports	Hit it long. Hit it straight
Sky Bet	Nothing's certain, that's why it's exciting
SuperCasino.com	Feel it for real
William Hill	The home of betting

GARDENING

AL-KO	Quality for life
Alitex	Aluminium made beautiful *But the aluminium greenhouse is lost in the slogan*
Amdega [conservatories]	A British design classic
Ark Wildlife	for a garden full of life
B&Q	Let's do it together
Bayer Garden	For feel good gardens, we can help
Coblands	Direct from the grower since 1963 *This slogan tries to make a double whammy – first, its distinctive feature; second, its age (like many watchmakers)*
Courtyard Designs	1) Buildings of distinction 2) Often imitated. Rarely matched. Never surpassed
Easigrass	The artificial grass company
Einhell	Quality tools at affordable prices
eSeeds.com	12,000 Varieties, 50 Brands, 1 Site
Everest	Fit the best

Gabriel Ash [greenhouses]	Naturally Superior Quality
Gold Leaf [gardening gloves]	Gloves for people serious about gardening
Hartley Botanic	Nothing else is a Hartley
Hayter	Makers of the finest mowers
HCL (Hammersmith and Chiswick Landscapes)	A passion for gardens
Hobbycraft	Handmade by you. Inspired by . . . Hobbycraft
Jacksons Fencing	Quality that lasts
John Deere	Commitment. It's in my blood *Far too non-specific*
Kärcher	Makes a difference
Miracle Gro Compost	It's grow time
Miracle Gro Patch Magic	Makes patches disappear like magic
Oak Leaf [garden rooms]	Designed and built for year round enjoyment
Patio Magic	The fountain of youth for patio furnishings* *Amongst often dull slogans, the word "fountain of youth" stands out*
Premier Polytunnels	The outside, inside *Nicely spelled out*
Robert Dyas	Bringing value home
Roundup	Kills weeds & roots
Royal Botania	Outdoor luxury
Schüco	Green Technology for the Blue Planet

SMC	Natural Insect Eliminator
STIHL	Relax, there's a STIHL for every job
Toro	Count on it
Viking Lawn Mowers (STIHL Group)	Innovation and quality for your garden *The "never underestimate a Viking" which accompanies their ads is more powerful, but it seems to belong to IKEA for their drawer lights*
Weedol	Fast acting weed killer
Westbury Garden Rooms	The future your home deserves
Westland	Garden Health

HANDBAGS, LUGGAGE

Aspinal of London	Elegant, sophisticated and uniquely distinctive *This definition, on their site, is more a description than a slogan – which is sadly missing for this company*
Asprey	Asprey, with love
Brahmin	Redefining timeless style *This slogan might be more appropriate for a watch*
Coach	Have a Coach Holiday
Cox & Kings	Relax & Explore
Delsey	Born to move* *Really nice: gets to the point in 10 letters*
Fendi	*Je le veux* (in French: I want it)
Gucci	Quality is remembered long after the price is forgotten
Hermès	1) Contemporary artisan since 1837 *Compare with many watchmaker slogans* 2) When tools meet inspiration

Kipling [handbags]	Carry your life with you
Louis Vuitton	*Certains voyages se transforment en légendes* (in French: there are journeys that turn into legends)
William & Son	Celebrating our first 10 years

HEALTHCARE [SEE ALSO "COSMETICS" AND "PHARMACEUTICALS"]

Abermed	Your health is our occupation
Addictions UK	Just a phone call away from addictions recovery *In spite of its clumsy nature, this slogan deserves its place in this book*
Betterfatloss.com	A better way to lose weight
Weight Watchers	Because it works

HORSES

Absorbine	The Horse World's most trusted name
Alexanders Horseboxes	Where dreams become reality
Baileys Horse Feeds	Experts in our field
British Horse Feeds	Trust the experts
Charles Britton	Quality that speaks for itself
Chestnut Horse Feeds	Suppliers of the unique bulk bin feeding system
CoolStance (Stance Equire)	Premium copra meal

Cortaflex	The UK's No 1 Equine joint supplement
Courchevel [horseboxes]	Horseboxes of distinction...
Dodson & Horrell	Horse Feed specialists
Elite Stallions	It's all about you!
Empire Horseboxes	Equine coachbuilders
Future Sport Horses	Breeding future champions
Fyna-lite	Serious tools for serious work
Galloper Horseboxes	A new dawn
Gersemi	The equestrian fashion brand
GWF Nutrition	Celebrating 40 years
Kingsland	Exceeding your expectations
NAF	Restoring the balance
Pfizer	Animal health
Pliance	Sensing body contact *All is said in those three words; a nice slogan*
QuitKick	Make door kicking a thing of the past!
Thorowgood	Saddles that fit
Tredstep	Elegance and performance
Vettec	Hoof care

HOTELS, RESORTS [SEE ALSO "TRAVEL", "TOURISM"]

Adriatic Luxury Hotels	Croatia's finest hotel collection
Banyan Tree, Phuket	Nothing comes close
Beacon [suppliers]	Altogether better
Best Western	1) Best Western The World's Largest Hotel Chain 2) Across the street from the ordinary *Compare with second Ramada slogan*
Casna Group	Redefining gold standards ...
Cateys [award]	Recognize. Reward. Celebrate
Cavendish Hotel	escape relax unwind
Christie & Co	Business Intelligence
Conrad Hotels & Resorts	The luxury of being yourself
Constance Hotels, Mauritius	Elegance comes naturally
Corinthia Hotel, London	The 21st century Grand Hotel
Cosmopolitan Hotel, Las Vegas	Just the right amount of wrong* *Nicely provocative*
Crowne Plaza	Sleep Advantage
Domes of Elounda, Crete	Dream with your eyes wide open
Embassy Suites Hotels	Everything for a reason
Four Seasons	1) Defining the art of service at 40 hotels in 19 countries *See RJ Reynolds in "Tobacco"* 2) Fifty hotels. Twenty-two countries. One philosophy *The numbers have increased, but the unwieldiness of the slogan hasn't decreased*

3) Not the usual
Better

4) When life seems perfect

Fullerton Bay Hotel, Singapore   Where heritage meets luxury

Grace Hotels   Amazing Grace

Halcyon Interiors   Celebrating thirty years

Hilton Hotels   1) Take me to the Hilton

2) The places you'd rather be

Holiday Inn   1) Relax, it's Holiday Inn

2) We put a smile back on your face

3) Pleasing people the world over

4) Stay You
I think the slogan tries to say "Be yourself", but doesn't succeed

Holiday Inn Express   Stay smart*
Rather good and definitely stronger than the slogans of the parent chain

Hotel Euler, Basel   Euler. It's not a hotel, it's a way of life

Hyatt   Feel the Hyatt touch
Ressembles the Royal Monceau, Paris slogan

InterContinental   1) One world, one hotel
Used to be "One world, One touch, Uniquely InterContinental". Vastly improved

2) We know what it takes*
Nice

3) Do you live an InterContinental life?
Suffers from the "query" form

Jumeirah   Stay different

Karkloof Spa, Sth Africa   Wellness & Wildlife Retreat

Langham Hotel, Hong Kong   Legend inspires Legend
Quite good

LateRooms.com	Dizzy with choice
Leading Hotels of the World	Every quest has a beginning *The problem here is that the trademark itself is already partly a slogan, because of the word "Leading"*
Lifehouse spa	Love life at Lifehouse
The Mandala, Berlin	Your home away from home* *Excellent*
Mandarin Oriental	She's a fan *Requires that the ad shows a woman – though can be easily adapted to masculine*
Mandarin Oriental, Hyde Park	Where nothing is overlooked except Hyde Park* *A double negative, implying that there is indeed a view of Hyde Park*
Marriott	1) When you're comfortable, you can do anything 2) Your Marriott awaits *Take on "Your chariot awaits"* 3) Your home away from home
MGM Hotels	One more reason to escape
The Mira, Hong Kong	Exceeding your expectations
Mövenpick [hotel]	Passionately Swiss
Novotel	Designed for natural living
One & Only Resorts	Live the moment
Park Inn (Radisson)	Adding colour to life
The Peninsula, Beverly Hills	The details make the Peninsula
Premier Inn	Everything's premier but the price *A bit clumsy*

Ramada	1) Ramada. A very good place to be 2) [R International] Everything except excess *Not too exciting – many hotel guests dream of excess in their favour*
Regalian	Quality in a word
Renaissance Hotels	1) It's time for a Renaissance* *Nice pun* 2) Be immersed 3) A new discovery, every time
The Ritz-Carlton	Where joy has no expiration date *I would have preferred "pleasure" to "joy"*
Rotana	There's one for you
Royal Monceau, Paris	Luxury with the French touch *Resembles Hyatt*
St Regis, Bal Harbour	Inspired living. Unrivalled address
Sarova Hotels	Individual hotels for individual people
Seasons Hotels	We live the places you'll love
The Sentosa, Singapore	Minutes away, worlds apart
Shangri-La	1) It must be Shangri-La 2) Be kind to your world
Sheraton	1) See for yourself 2) Who's taking care of you?
Small Luxury Hotels	Experience another world
Sofitel	Life is *Magnifique* *A good mix of languages*
Starwood Preferred Guest (Starwood Hotels)	Be one** *Great*
Sunlight	Textile services
Swire Hotels	Individuality is in House

Sysco	Good things come from Sysco
Travelodge	Sleep tight
Westin	1) Modern luxury *Seems to express all you need in a good hotel; and yet . . .* 2) Westin. Choose your travel partner wisely

HOUSEHOLD [SEE ALSO "FURNITURE"]

ADT	Always there
AEG	Perfekt in form und funktion *Practically in German*
Air Wick	1) Fragrances that change your world 2) Something in the Air Wick *Somewhat far-fetched but ok if one lets one's imagination roam*
Alessi	The useful art
Alno	Generation kitchen
Alternative Plans	Uncompromisingly modern designs for kitchens and bathrooms
Andrex	It's the little things
Ariel	Brrrrrilliant *Neat, but might be misleading, since the "brrrr" evokes shivering in the cold*
Armstrong	Your ideas become reality
Artemide [lighting]	The human light
Arthur Price	Enduring Perfection, for Today and Tomorrow
Aston Matthews	Established 1823

Axminster Carpets

Natural. British. Beautiful
A rare nationalistic slogan

Bang & Olufsen

Everything is possible
Identical to the Hewlett-Packard one. See also Adidas

Barlow Tyrie

Quality since 1920

Bathstore

Eureka!
A great reference to Archimedes and his discoveries in the bath

Bette

Natürlich im Bad (in German: bathrooms naturally)

Bissell

Experts in home cleaning

Black & Decker

Your floor is clean, really clean
This is a jab at other cleaners, of course

Bosch

Invented for life
Too vague – could refer to any type of product

Bose

Better sound through research

Brabantia

Solid company
Maybe a clothes dryer does need to have the word "solid" to promote it

Brawny [paper towels]

Premium performance

Brita

Your source at home

Calgon

Washing machines live longer with Calgon

Carini Lang

Carpets with soul*
Nice, because suddenly your carpet becomes alive

Casamance

Fine fabrics

Cascade

The best clean ever

Cavalio

For contemporary living

Chalon

Finest quality handmade kitchens

Chesney's	The world's most beautiful fireplaces and stoves
Chinet	Cut crystal
Cif	Always a beautiful ending. Easily
Cillit Bang	Bang and the dirt is gone
Clas Ohlson	From homeware to hardware since 1918
Clorox	Momma's got the magic of Clorox *This slogan has been attacked as discriminatory against women*
Coopers of Stortford	Traditional service, great value
Corian	Solid surfaces
Cotteswood	Makers of English kitchen furniture
C.P. Hart	The source of bathroom inspiration
Cranbrook Basements	There's valuable space beneath your feet
Cushelle [toilet tissue]	Irresistibly soft
Daz	The soap you can believe in
Deirdre Dyson	Bespoke contemporary handmade carpets
De'Longhi	1) Living innovation 2) To be an occasion, it must be shared
Diversey	For a cleaner, healthier future
Dolphin	From start to finishing touch
Domestos	1) Total toilet cleaning system 2) Kills germs as it freshens

Dornbracht	The SPIRIT of WATER
Drummonds	Classic handmade quality
Dulux	Let's colour
Dwell	Live like this
Dyson Air Multiplier	No blades. No buffeting
Dyson Cleaner	The cleaner that doesn't lose suction
Edwins [bathrooms]	Design solutions on your doorstep
Eggersmann	Sophisticated since 1905
Elg Ltd	Creating fine furnishings since 1918
Fairy	1) Trust Fairy to make it easy
	2) Soften your world
	Great
Farrow & Ball [paints]	1) Colour craftsmen since 1946
	This phrase, like several ones before, is more a statement of long age than a true slogan – compare with certain watchmaker slogans
	2) Great recipes deserve great ingredients
	Without wanting to be overly critical, the word "recipe" immediately makes the consumer think of food, even though some of the paint names do refer to food, such as "dead salmon"
Febreze	1) It's a breath of fresh air
	2) Thirty days of continuous freshness
Finish [dishwasher tablets]	The diamond standard
Gaggenau	The difference is Gaggenau
Geberit	The WC that cleans you with water

Glade [air freshener]   Discreet
*It seems that the word "discreet" is used
simultaneously as an adjective for the freshener
and as a slogan*

Glade [candles]   Relaxing moments

GPlan [upholstery]   Great past. Great present. Great
future
*And . . . great slogan, were it not for its lack of
specificity*

Graham & Brown   Making the walls of Britain great

Graham and Green   For the super stylish

Granite Transformations   The top that fits on top

Häcker   Kitchen German Made
*At the very limit of a slogan – more like a
statement*

Haier   So easy

Harrods Home   The finest interiors from outside
the world

Harvey Jones Kitchens   Handmade for living

Hillarys   The home of blinds and shutters

Home Depot   Driving down the cost of home
improvement

Homebase   Make a/your house a home

Hoover   Generation Future
*One of the surprisingly very few slogans to use
the word "future"; see MasterCard and Texas
Instruments*

**Hotpoint [washing
machines]**   Our ideas. Your home

Howdens Joinery   Making space more valuable

iRobot   Making Robots work for you

Karndean   Design flooring

Kenmore   That's genius

Kin Knives   Kin sharp
In British slang "kin" means "fucking"

Kohler   The bold look of Kohler*
*One of the rare cases where repetition of the
company name brings a huge plus*

Kohl's   The more you know the more you
Kohl's

Kohro   Inspiring interiors

Krups   Beyond reason
*In itself, a beautiful slogan – but seems
inappropriate for a coffee machine*

La Cornue   Where exceptional taste begins

Lakeland   The home of creative kitchenware

Landmark Lofts   Raising the benchmark

Le Creuset   I dream of beauty

Leisure [range cookers]   Love food. Love Leisure

Lenox   American by design

Lladró   1) A language more powerful than
words
2) A tradition of beauty will last
forever

Magimix [toaster]   Built better to last longer

Magnet   What happens in your
kitchen?
*Remarked as quite daring when published,
since it said nothing about what Magnet
provides or does*

Marston & Langinger   1) Individually designed.
Individually made
2) Extraordinary garden rooms

Matki Showering	Pure Matki
Mercury [cookers]	Designed for perfection
Miele	1) Anything else is a compromise *Very close to having a star; but slightly aggressive towards the competition* 2) Forever better *These two words do convey duration and quality; pretty good* 3) Everyone deserves a Miele
Mira Showers	Showering perfection
MMM	Innovation
Moben	Clever kitchens designed around you *Resembles another slogan where the building starts around the central owner, ie Barrett Homes*
Morris & Co.	Celebrating 150 years of design
Mowlem & Co.	Inspirational furniture
Neff	Writing kitchen history
Neptune	Kitchen / Interior / Garden
OzKleen	Great at kleening (not so good at spelling)* *Slogan and subslogan full of fun*
P&G (Procter and Gamble)	1) Touching lives, improving life 2) Proud sponsors of mums 3) Professional *This nice single-word term is really more a sub-division of P&G than a slogan*
The Packhouse	Stylish vintage living
Patrick Gaguech	*De l'amour du détail naît la perfection* (in French: from the love of detail, perfection is born)
Persil	Small and mighty *A take on the 1954* The High and Mighty *movie*

Poggenpohl	Knowing what counts
Quick-Step [floors]	Discover a world you'd love to live in
Quooker	1) Quooker is quicker! 2) The boiling-water tap
Rangemaster	Britain's No. 1 range cooker
Renova	The black toilet paper company *Daring – though the ad itself; "the sexiest paper on earth" would have been great too*
Renuzit	Subtle effects *Very classy for such a difficult topic as a bathroom deodorant*
Ripples	Our forecast is for more showers across the country** *What a superb play on bathroom showers and weather showers!*
Roca	The leading global bathroom brand
Rocky Mountain [hardware]	Handcast Solid Bronze
Ronseal	Does exactly what it says on the tin
Rust-Oleum	Trusted quality since 1921
SA Baxter	1) Where architecture begins 2) Architectural hardware
Samuel Heath	For a life less ordinary
Savers	health, home & beauty
SC Johnson	A family company
Scott [toilet paper]	Common sense on a roll *Great pun*
SEBO	The floorcare professionals
Shout OxyPower	More oxygen power to shout it out

Siemens	The future moving in
Silestone	The Original
Smeg	Technology with style
Stannah	Not all stairlifts are the same. This one certainly isn't
Stovax & Gazco	Fire your imagination *If fireplaces were as popular as computers, this slogan would have a worldwide reputation*
Sub-zero	A sub-zero is just a refrigerator, like a diamond is just a stone *Too long-winded, and the comparison questionable. Compare with Wolf*
Swarovski [see also "Jewellery, Watches"]	Discover the magic of crystal
Sylvania	Brilliant light
TC Bathrooms	Immerse your senses
Ted Shred's [candles]	The scent of surfing
Tempur	And so to bed** *Rather . . . tempting and implies that everything is perfect; a very Gallic slogan!*
Thermomix	Your extra pair of hands!
Thomas Sanderson [window shutters]	An expression of individuality
Turkish Ceramics	Timeless! *Justified by their having existed for eight millennia*
Turtle Mat	Practically perfect
Vanish	Trust pink, forget stains *One of the rare cases where the colour of the packaging – the plastic bottle, here – is used in a slogan*

Vanish Sensitive	Tough on stains. Gentle on skin
Vax	Performance is everything
Velux	Bringing light to life* *A beauty*
Victoria Plumb	The online bathroom store
Waterford	1) Live a crystal life 2) The sparkle of a new beginning
Wedgwood	At home in the finest homes
Wesley-Barrel	A lasting future
Whirlpool	Just imagine *I do imagine – and I don't necessarily relate to this particular company*
Wickes	It's got our name on it
Wolf	A Wolf is just an oven, like a diamond is just a stone *I would have preferred something simpler, like "Put a diamond in your kitchen". Compare with Sub-zero*
Wyndham	Bespoke
Zepter International	Striving for a longer life
Zip Hydro Tap	Instant boiling water

INSURANCE, RETIREMENT, SECURITY

ACE	25 years of insuring progress *A clever play on the words "insurance", "insuring"*
Admiral.com	One premium. One renewal. One policy.

Aetna	1) You'll feel better with us
	2) Turning promise into practice
Aflac	Without it, no insurance is complete
AIG	World leaders in insurance and financial services
	A description of the company rather than a slogan
Allianz	The power beside you
	Not far from deserving a star
Allstate	1) You're in good hands
	2) Dollar for dollar, nobody protects you like Allstate
AON	Insure your future
Aviva	Forward thinking
	At first sounds a bit too abstract; at second thought, not so bad
AXA	1) Go ahead
	2) Be life confident
	3) Redefining standards
Best Life Cover	We search. You save
	Good
Bupa	1) BUPA. Feel better
	2) Helping you find healthy
Canada Life	Small things grow great
Capital Re [insurance]	Re
	Sourceful
Centor	Insurance and risk management
Chubb	1) Life is too short to worry about possessions
	2) Chubb. Without question

Cigna	A business of caring
Cincinnati Financial	Making your strength your future
Columbusdirect.com	The traveller's best friend
Directline.com	Making insurance straightforward
E & L [horse, rider and trailer insurance]	The Niche Insurance Specialists
Elephant.co.uk	Seriously good car insurance
Fidelity [see also "Personal Finance"]	1) Smart move 2) Turn here
Fidelity.com	Every second counts *Good, but could apply to practically any business in the world*
Fireman's Fund (Allianz)	License to get on with it *Somewhat obscure*
FM (Factory Mutual) Global	Securing the future of your business
Guardian	The intelligent choice
Hartford	1) Bring it on 2) Always thinking ahead
Hiscox	As good as our word
insureandgo.com	Feeding your passion for travel
John Lewis Home Insurance	We're with you when it matters
Kemper	Insurance for today's world
Liberty Mutual	The freedom of Liberty
MetLife	Have you met life today? *Nice pun*
New York Life	The company you keep

NFU Mutual	We do right by you
Northwestern Mutual Life	The Quiet Company
OnStar	Wherever you go, here we are
Quantum	Exceptional Personal Insurance
Reliance	How can we be so old and move so fast?
RIAS	1) Because experience has its rewards 2) Where insurance gets better with age
Royal Insurance	You have our attention
Saga	Insurance done properly
SCOR	The art and science of risk
Scottish Widows	My money works *The word "money" is in red*
Simplyhealth	We *can* be bothered
State Farm	Like a good neighbor State Farm is there
Swiss Life	1) The right decision 2) *Vous avancez, nous assurons* (in French: you advance, we ensure)
TIAA-CREF	Ensuring the future for those who shape it
UL	Working for a safer world
Windsor Meade	Retirement history in the making
Zurich	1) Building relationships, solution by solution

2) Because change happenz
*Not bad – but if they really wanted to put a "z"
instead of an "s", there were other ways:
"inzurance", for instance*

**Zurich American
Insurance Group**

The power of partnership

INTERNET, NETWORKS [SEE ALSO "COMMUNICATIONS", "COMPUTING"]

3Com

More connected

ANS Group

The Internet just got serious

AOL (America Online)

1) So easy to use, no wonder it's #1
See US Robotics

2) Time to lighten up
*Quite good; on the internet things will be easier
and lighter*

Cabletron Systems

Your e-business communications
specialist

Cisco

1) Powered network
*Rather pale imitation of Intel "inside", since it
describes itself*

2) Empowering the Internet
generation
*Not much better, but does have the audacious
use of verb "empower"*

3) Welcome to the human network
*At last, a nice one! A variant is "Together we are
the human network"*

Cnet.com

The source for computers and
technology

Comcast

We never stop making fast faster

Datapipe

Your Competitive Edge

Ebuyer.com

Technology delivered

Expansys	Be first
Fasthosts	World Class Virtual Servers
IBM	E-business is the game. Play to win
Infonet	1) More than a connection 2) Insight matters
Inquisit	Opportunity doesn't knock. It emails* *A very nice way of introducing contemporary technology into a slogan*
Jupiter Communications	Online intelligence
Level 3	The network partner you can rely on
Logitech	Designed to move you
MSN.8	More useful everyday *Compare with Household and with Martha Stewart*
NET.com	We put the net to work for you
PlayOn	Engage your senses
Siemens I&C	1) Be inspired *But see also Hammonds and Mark Wilkinson furniture companies* 2) Intelligent solutions for a powerful market *Too lengthy; why not "As intelligent as powerful"?*
Sprint	Get there with Sprint
VeriSign	The value of trust

JEWELLERY AND WATCHES

A. Lange & Söhne	For people who would never, ever wear a digital watch *Somewhat negative slogan – doesn't give the positives of the watch*

Adler

1) *Mémoires de femmes. Mémoire du monde* (in French: remembrance of women, remembrance of the world)
2) Jewellers since 1886
Compare with several watchmakers

Armani

Style that defines the time

Audemars Piguet

1) *Le maître de l'horlogerie depuis 1875* (in French: master watchmaker since 1875)
2) The master watchmaker

Backes & Strauss

Masters of diamonds since 1789

Baume & Mercier

1) Time is mine
2) Life is about moments

Bell & Ross

Time instruments

Boodles

British Excellence since 1798

Breguet

Depuis 1775 (in French: since 1775)

Breitling

1) A passion for perfection*
Very neat, with a quasi-alliteration; much better than the second slogan
2) Instruments for professionals

Bulgari

The essence of a jeweller

Bulova

1) Keeping America's time for generations
2) Designed to be noticed

Cartier

1) 150 years of history and romance
2) True love has a colour and a name
Not certain that this is a slogan, though it appears as the bottom statement on a recent full-page ad by Cartier; whatever the case the slogan could be shortened by taking away the word "colour"

Chamilia

Your life. Your style

Chaumet	1) *Joailliers depuis 1780* (in French: jewellers since 1780)
	2) Creating watches for 200 years
	Even an outstandingly classy company like Chaumet hasn't resisted the trend of having a slogan – although it still refers to the company's age
ChloBo	Irresistibly Collectable Jewellery
Chopard	The ultimate reference
Citizen	How the world tells time
Concord	The sensation of time
Corum	1) *La passion de créér* (in French: the passion of creating)
	2) Swiss timepieces
Damiani	A girl's best friend
	With the word "girl" (contradicted somewhat by the photo in the ad) the company sets itself up as jeweller for younger women
David Morris	There is only one
De Beers	A diamond is forever**
	This motto is so well-known that it is part of our daily language
DeWitt	Classical audacity
Ebel	The architects of time*
	Rather good because it has both the idea of time and of construction of the watch
ESQ (Movado)	Every second counts*
	A nice slogan, particularly if you are in a hurry
Folli Follie	Girls just want to have fun!
Fortunoff	The source for the elegant to the extraordinary
Franck Muller	Master of complications*
	A great way to take pride in something normally reprehensible

Fréderique Constant	Live your passion
Gabriel & Co	Passion. Love. Gabriel
Garrard	The Crown Jeweller
Georg Jensen	Outrageously Scandinavian since 1904 *Possibly they had a simpler one in 2004!*
Gerald Genta	The living legend
Graaff Diamonds	1) Unmistakably** *Again the great strength of a well-chosen single word* 2) Today, time begins* *Very thought provoking* 3) The most fabulous jewels in the world *Far more down to earth*
Harry Winston	1) The ultimate timepiece 2) Rare timepieces 3) Live the moment
Hearts on Fire	The world's most perfectly cut diamond
IWC	Since 1868. And for as long as there are men
Jaeger-LeCoultre	Rendez-Vous at the heart of time
Jewellery Channel	Make every day sparkle
Les Ambassadeurs	The leading house of leading names
Leviev	Extraordinary diamonds *A sales pitch rather than a slogan*
Longines	1) *L'élégance du temps depuis 1832* (in French: the elegance of time since 1832) 2) Elegance is an attitude
Michael Rose	Source of the unusual

Mikimoto	The sensation of pearls
Movado	1) The art of time
	2) The art of design
	How should we judge this change of one word? The first slogan is preferred because it tells us that a watch is involved
Nomination [Italy]	Live. Love. Life
Novo	It's all about you
OMEGA	The sign of excellence
Oris	Enduring
	I would have preferred "Endearing. Enduring"
Pandora	Unforgettable moments
Panerai	1) *Laboratorio di idee* (in Italian: a lab of ideas/where ideas come to life)
	2) History always leaves a trace
	Excellent; of course there is the trace recorded by the watch, but this sentence also has a meaning of general importance
	3) The simplicity of innovation
Parmigiani	Heritage in the making
Patek Philippe	1) Begin your own tradition
	Initial italics on "own" have disappeared
	2) Begin an enduring love affair
	This slogan, aimed at female clients, loses through the final word what it gains by evoking love (in French: Le début d'une longue histoire d'amour)
Piaget	1) *Joaillier en horlogerie depuis 1874* (in French: watchwork jewellery since 1874)
	2) One watch. Three positions to play with
	In spite of the grandiose photos, not so easy to understand that the slogan refers to the rewind knob
	3) Jewellery in motion
Platinum	Pure. Rare. Eternal

Pulsar — Tell it your way

Rado — Unlimited spirit

Richard Mille
1) Richard Mille, *des montres à 300.000 euros* (in French: Richard Mille, watches for 300,000 euros)
What might look like just a boastful slogan is truly excellent, because it does set apart this particular watch company from others – by the price tag
2) A racing machine on the wrist

Rolex
1) Perpetual spirit*
The word "perpetual" has a double meaning here, implying also that the watch never stops
2) In time with [the logo] Rolex
3) A crown for every achievement
Refers to the Rolex logo, shaped as a crown; yet note that there is only one crown in the logo drawing, whereas the slogan itself implies many . . .
4) For life's defining moments
5) Live for greatness

Seiko — Dedicated to perfection

Steuben Glass — Timeless. Elegant. American

Storywheels — What's your life story?

Susan Astaire — Affordable luxury

Suzy K — Designer jewellery with a sporting theme

Swarovski — See the Wonder . . . Feel the brilliance . . . Touch the world
Obviously too long-winded

Swarovski Aura — The luminescent fragrance. The dazzling make-up jewels

Swatch — Shake the world

Swiss Army — Life ahead of you. A legacy behind you

TAG Heuer	1) Swiss Avant-Garde since 1860 2) Beyond measure 3) What are you made of? 4) History begins every morning* *Good allusion to the daily winding of one's watch*
Tiffany & Co.	1) New York since 1837 *Compare with several watchmakers' slogans* 2) Some style is legendary 3) There are times to celebrate 4) Give voice to your heart
Timex	One more time
Tissot	1) Take care of details 2) Innovators by tradition* *A good mix of the past and the future*
Triton	Where art meets engineering
Trollbeads	Discover your essence
Tudor	Designed for performance. Engineered for excellence *Too lengthy*
TW Steel	Big in oversized watches *Not bad at all – they don't shy from emphasising the point*
Ulysse Nardin	Since 1846
Vacheron Constantin	The oldest watch manufacturer in the world
Van Cleef & Arpels	1) *Croire en ses rêves et un jour les réaliser* (in French: to believe in one's dreams and one day make them come true) 2) The poetry of time

Wittnauer	Passionate about elegance
Zenith	The pioneer spirit since 1865

LEGAL

Bingham	The tougher the deal the more we enjoy it* *A rather exciting slogan, purposely lengthy, and yet highly original; remains in the mind*
First4lawyers	Find the right lawyer for you
Injurylawyers4u.co.uk	Free honest advice
Pinsent Masons	Think pensions . . . think Pinsents

LOGISTICS

APL	We know how and why
CF Companies	We put you miles ahead
CNF	Where ideas carry weight
DHL	1) We keep your promises 2) We move the world** *Really excellent: short strong words, and conveys the entire meaning of the company's field* 3) Excellence. Simply delivered *Not as good as the previous one*
Federal Express	Don't worry. There's a Fedex for that
Fuchs	Committed to move your world
International Paper	We answer to the world
Mail Boxes Etc.	Send it our way
NYK Line [Japan]	We still navigate by the stars
Public Transportation	Wherever life takes you

United States Postal Service	We deliver
UPS	1) Consider it done** *A daring credo, which goes straight at alleviating the anxiety of the potential customer; also compare with Unisys slogan – which has the unfortunate full stop between the first two words and third* 2) Moving at the speed of business 3) What can Brown do for you?
VIAG AG	Creating enduring value

MANAGEMENT SERVICES

Advantest	You can test. Or you can Advantest
Clarify	All you need to know
Hewitt	For 18 million clients
Hyundai	Building a better world through value management
Kelly Services	Look what we do now
Kudos	The information company
Mercer	Based on reality
Mississippi	Business solutions for a new millennium
Norrell	Strategic workforce management
Tivoli Management (IBM)	The Power To Manage. Anything. Anywhere
Viasoft	Managing the business of information technology

MEDIA [SEE ALSO "COMMUNICATIONS"]

Barron's   News before the market knows

BBC   1) You make it what it is*

Although this slogan could be applied to many companies, it does imply interaction between the channels and their audience – and it's powerful. Too bad the BBC abandoned it

2) Perfect day

3) This is what we do

BBC World News   1) Demand a broader view

2) Making sense of it all

3) Putting news first

Bertelsmann AG   The spirit to create

Bloomberg BusinessWeek   1) Watch. Wherever you are

2) Beyond news. Intelligence

CNBC   1) Profit from it

2) First in business worldwide

A far better slogan

3) Make it your business

4) Capitalize on it

Very close to the first one

CNN   1) Be the first to know

Not bad; insists on the speed of CNN news; almost deserves a star

2) The world's news leader

Somewhat immodest, whether true or not

3) Go beyond borders

Country Life [magazine]   The home of premium property

Nice articulation between the magazine as a "home" and their subject matter, properties on sale

Daily Express   You want change. Change today

The Economist	1) Make an impression
	2) Independent. International. Indispensable
	Misses a star because, in spite of the nice repetition, no allusion to a journal
ESPN	1) The worldwide leader in sports
	2) Miss nothing*
	In spite of two negatives, not bad
EuroBusiness [magazine]	Because business doesn't stop at borders
Evening Standard	Know what London's thinking
Financial Times	No FT, no comment
First [women's magazine]	First. The conversation starts here
Food and Travel Magazine	Taste the experience – experience the taste
	Rather good
Forbes	1) The world is ready. Are you?
	2) Forbes Capitalist tool
	Nicely provocative, because "capitalist" has become a pejorative word!
Fortune [magazine]	1) We're committed to you
	2) Younger and wiser
Free	Buy today. Watch today. Free forever
Grazia	Have you got your GRAZIA?
History Channel	Where the past comes alive
International Herald Tribune	The world's daily newspaper
ITV1	The brighter side
	Has a take on both the brightness of a TV screen and the innovative comments
Magazines	The power of print
NBC Europe	Where the stars come out at night

NBC News   When you really want to know

New York Times   All the news that's fit to print
So famous it's difficult to evaluate this slogan

Newsweek   The international news magazine

Restaurant [magazine]   Says it all

Resurgence [magazine]   Celebrating 45 years

Reuters [before merger]   1) Know Now**
Superbly short and rhythmic – and the first word has the second one inside it!
2) New era. New tools

Sky   Believe in better

The Spectator   1) Champagne for the brain*
Not only is it persuasive via the use of the word "champagne", but also it manages to make reference to the field it is talking about – an intellectual one
2) Don't think alike

Sport [magazine]   The weekend starts here

Stuff   The world's best-selling gadget magazine

Sunday Times   1) Sunday isn't Sunday without the *Sunday Times*
2) For all you are
This somewhat mysterious phrase "recognises that we are multi-dimensional people with a host of interests and passions"

SurfGirl   Swing into Spring

Tatler   What fun!

Thomson Reuters [after merger]   Knowledge to act

Time   1) Step out of your world
2) Join the conversation*
Nicely to the point
3) Know where

The Times	Be part of the time*
	Nice invention, with a not-too-insistent play on the word "time"
TV	Where brands get their break**
	A jewel! Not only is the story of the poor forlorn dog which accompanies this ad fabulous, but here the rhyming between "brands" and "break" is effortless but persuasive
US News and World Report	News you can use
	Great rhyme
Vogue	1) *Vogue* – for the overwhelming minority
	2) If it wasn't in VOGUE, it wasn't in vogue
	Excellent play on the "vogue" word itself, but why the past tense?
	3) Get it first. Get it fast
The Wall Street Journal	1) The daily diary of the American dream
	2) Every journey needs a journal
	In spite of the play on "journey" and "journal", this slogan does not single out the WSJ
	3) Live in the know*
	Great, albeit not specific to any journal; goes to show that good thinking ends up with a good slogan
World of Interiors	The ultimate design magazine
Yesterday [TV channel]	Where the past is always present*
	Lovely description of the purpose of the channel

MEDICAL RESEARCH, HOSPITALS [SEE ALSO "HEALTHCARE", "PHARMACEUTICALS"]

Barchester	Celebrating life
Dana-Farber Cancer Institute	Dedicated to discovery

Genentech	In business for life
Harley Medical Group	Inspiring confidence in you
Memorial Sloan-Kettering Cancer Center	The best cancer care. Anywhere
Royal Hospital for Neuro-disability	Thinking time *This is an ad asking for charity rather than boasting their research*
Trinity Hospice	Living every moment
Vision Express	We'll see you right *Good pun on the seeing by the company and that of the patient*

MINING

Anglo American	Real mining. Real people. Real difference* *Although lengthy, quite original, with the strong repeat of "Real"*
AngloGold Ashanti	One element runs rings around them all* *Again a double-edged slogan, with the gold ring and gold "running rings around", or dominating, the other elements; but a bit lengthy*
Freeport-McMoRan	A natural leader

OFFICE AND SCHOOL SUPPLIES

Cross	Unexpectedly Cross
Epson	Exceed your vision
Lamy	The desire to write
Lyreco	You're our number One!

Montblanc	1) The art of writing *This slogan grows on you* 2) A story to tell *Maybe not quite as good as the first one*
MWB Business Exchange	Address to impress
Oxford	Write it. Make it
Parker	1) A Parker is in the details 2) Write your own story
Ricoh	We're in your corner
Samsung	1) Everyone's invited 2) Turn on tomorrow *Possibly the best of the lot* 3) Live life on your terms 4) Where the possible begins 5) Use your influence 6) Imagine the possibilities *This list of slogans, all of them quite good, shows that it's relatively easy to come up with a good short slogan but more difficult to create one which stays in everyone's mind*
Samsung Notebook	Designed to go. Powered to perform
Sharp	1) From sharp minds come Sharp products* *A great use of the brand name, repeated twice with different meanings* 2) This is why *A beautiful slogan per se, but says nothing about the nature of the company. I might add, ironically: "Why this slogan?"*
Stabilo	The easy handwriting pen for school
Staples	That was easy! *Interesting slogan using the past tense*
Tipp-Ex	White and rewrite *A nice try on the rhyme*
Viking	All the inspiration your office needs

Wilkhahn	Chassis for work and life
Xerox	1) The document company
	Although not very evocative, likely to become catching
	2) Ready for Real Business

ONLINE SERVICES

Allaboutyou.com	Smart women click here
	An easy-going good slogan
Goodgaragescheme.com	It's like having a friend in the know
Jobsite.co.uk	Our job is searching for your job
Lovestruck.com	Where busy people click
Match.com	Make love happen
Mazuma.com	Turn your old mobile into cash
Motors.co.uk	Your search ends here
MyTrack	Trade like a Pro
Suretrader.com	The smart tool for smart investors
Webuyanycar.com	The UK's favourite specialist car buyer
Weightwatchers online	Finally, losing weight clicks
Wonga.com	1) Little loans, lot of control
	2) Straight talking money

PERSONAL FINANCE [SEE ALSO "FINANCIAL SERVICES"]

ABN AMRO	1) The network bank
	2) Making more possible
Ally Bank	Straightforward

Bank of America	1) Power in motion
	2) Embracing ingenuity *More to the point than the first slogan*
Bankers Trust	Architects of value
Barclays	1) Fluent in finance
	2) Being in control
	3) Take one small step *The word "step" is often shown above the other three words in the slogan*
BNP Paribas	1) Thinking beyond banking* *A rather astute slogan*
	2) The bank for a changing world
BNY Mellon [see also Mellon]	Who's helping you? *Although good, this slogan suffers, like similar ones, from the interrogative form*
Business Cash Advance	Unlocking your future sales potential
Centaur	Investment. Intelligence. Instruction
Chase	1) The right relationship is everything
	2) What matters
Citibank	The City never sleeps *Shortened to the more personalised "citi never sleeps"*
Citizens Bank	Not your typical bank
Commerzbank	German know-how in global finance
Crédit Lyonnais	Let's talk* *User-friendly*
Crédit Suisse	1) Whatever makes you happy
	2) True specialists
	3) It's time for an expert [Investment Consulting]

Deutsche Bank	1) Leading to results
	2) A passion to perform
	Vastly improved
Discover [credit cards]	It pays to switch. It pays to Discover
EFG International	Practitioners of the craft of private banking
Ethical Forestry	Sustainable timber investments
Fidelity	Bringing investing to life
First Direct	Banking is better in black and white
Fleming	Premier banking
Fortis (BNP Paribas)	Getting you there
Geneva Private Bankers	Liberty. Independence. Responsibility
GFT	Above all, integrity
Goldman Sachs	Progress is eveyone's business
Halifax	1) The people who give you extra
	2) A little extra help
Hanson Bank	A company over there that's doing rather well over here
HSBC	1) The world's local bank
	2) World class performers
Hypo Bank	Our energy is your capital
ING Direct	A decent way to do banking
Investec	Out of the ordinary
	Says nothing about the company . . . And the zebra logo even less . . .
LGT Bank, Liechtenstein	Expect more
	Pretty good; would be worth a star if there were some reference to banking
Janus	Go farther
Julius Baer Group	1) The fine art of private banking
	2) True to you

Lloyds TSB	For the journey . . .* *Rather fine; implies a lot while staying with the* *normal reserve of bankers . . .*
Lombard Odier & Cie	A different perspective for a bigger picture
Money Advice Service	Helping you feel good about money
Morgan Stanley	One client at a time* *Excellent, because it conveys perfectly the idea* *that each client is taken care of individually*
Nationwide	1) Proud to be different 2) On your side *It is not clear whether or not this slogan is an* *improvement*
NatWest	Helpful banking
Purple Loans	Add colour to your life
Rabobank Group	The power of knowledge
Republic National Bank of New York	Strength. Security. Service
Royal Bank of Scotland	Here for you
Santander	1) Value from ideas 2) Driven to do better
Schroder's	Sound investment thinking
Société Générale	Red, black and rising *Allusion to the two colours of the SG logo; in this* *slogan, the word "Red" is actually coloured red*
Syz & Co	Created to perform
UBS	1) The power of partnership 2) U & US *On the TV screen, the & U in the middle smartly* *transforms into a B and the slogan into UBS*
Wells Fargo	Together we'll go far
Zenith	In your best interest

PETROLEUM

BP

1) Beyond petroleum**
Outstanding since it repeats the initials and even keeps the second word of the company name; the first word change suffices to give the positive outlook. Compare with ACER slogan

2) Looking after the heart of your car
More explicit, less explosive

3) London 2012. Fuelling the future

Chevron

1) The symbol of partnership
2) Human energy
Petrol is not quite "human energy", really

Chevron Texaco

Turning partnership into energy

ERG

Where Italy finds energy

Mobil

The energy to make a difference
Close resemblance to Hewlett-Packard

Saudi Aramco

Energy to the world

Shell

1) Wave of change
Nice reference to the sea, where shells are found

2) Let's Go

Texaco

A world of energy

Total

1) Our energy is your energy*
Strong in spite of its length; to the point – energy – and implies sharing between company and customer

2) Our energy is without limits

PETS

ASPCA

Be part of our heart

Blue Cross

Britain's pet charity

Cesar	1) Sophisticated Food for Sophisticated Dogs* *Full of humour* 2) Love them back
Dreamies	The treat cats crave
Feliway	The secret to happy cats
Felix	Clever cats like Felix
Go-Cat	For kittens that live life to the full
Healthy Pets	The Pet Insurance Specialists
Hill's	Vet's no1 choice
Mayhew Animal Home	Helping animals and their carers since 1886
Purina	1) Bring out the champion in your dog 2) Your pet, our passion* *Excellent; four strong words, with repetition of the "p" – and says a lot about the purpose of the slogan while being very general* 3) The best ingredient is love

PHARMACEUTICALS [SEE ALSO "COSMETICS", "HEALTHCARE" AND "HOUSEHOLD"]

Abreva	Think fast. Think Abreva
Acuvue [contact lenses]	See what could be
Advair	Because life should take your air away. Not asthma
Advil	Advance to Advil *The alliteration is nice – but the slogan gives no hint of the company's field*

All About Weight	Fast, healthy weight loss
Allegra	Real relief. For real living
Allergan	The science of rejuvenation
Alli	How healthy works
Always	Have a happy period. Always* *Two puns here: a) on the word "period", which can simply mean time, or its more specific meaning; b) on the word "always", meaning either forever or the narrower company name*
Ambien	Works like a dream* *Great, since it conveys the idea that the medicine will make you sleep nicely*
Arm & Hammer	1) Switch to Arm & Hammer. You'll never go back *Sounds more like an ad than a slogan. However, could be easily shortened to a slogan* 2) The standard of purity
Astellas	Leading light for life
Avandia	Help use the natural insulin in you
Aveeno	Discover the power of active naturals
Aventis	Our challenge is life
Avon	There's a world out there
Bayer	Expertise with responsibility
Bazuka	Bazuka that Verruca . . . Bazuka that Wart
Benecol	Proven to lower cholesterol
Beyaz	Beyond birth control
Bimuno Travelaid	Support your tummy while abroad
BlanX	BlanX whitens naturally
Bonjela	Our most complete treatment ever

Boots	Feel good *Quite nice; had it been created 50 years ago,* *might be famous*
Cephalon	Insights into medicine
Chuan Spa	1) Captivate your senses 2) Rediscover your source *It seems the company needs an appropriate* *combination of the two to obtain its perfect* *slogan*
Cirrus	Have you heard?
Clarivu	Total vision correction
Colgate	Cleans more than just teeth
Compeed	Be unstoppable
Crest	Healthy, beautiful smiles for life
Decléor	Essential to beauty
Deep Freeze	Spray on. Play on* *Right to the point*
Dulcolax	Predictable overnight relief
Durex	Mutual pleasure *Although it is part of the brand name, it* *effectively functions as a slogan*
Elastoplast	When life gets exciting
Eucerin	Skin science that shows
Exorex	Effective psoriasis relief *For once I would say that the slogan is too* *explicit, by referring to a disease with* *pejorative implications*
Exuviance	The science of skin transformation
Fixodent	Best hold
Gaviscon	What a feeling!

Gillette	The best a man can get
Good Mood [tablets]	Have a Good Mood day!
Halls	Free your throat
Healthspan	Nutrition for a healthy lifespan
Hidden Hearing	We listen, you hear* *Excellent*
Hollis-Eden	Serving humanity
Ibuleve	Pain relief – without pills
Imodium	1) Faster relief than you can count on 2) Fast but gentle *Much better*
Johnson & Johnson	The family company
Lactofree	Dump the lactose, not the dairy
Listerine	Cleans where brushing misses
Lloyds Pharmacy	Health care for life
LoveLula.com	The organic apothecary
Merck	Committed to bringing out the best in Medicine
Miravant	Medical technologies
MSD [known as Merck in USA and Canada]	Where patients come first
Mylan	Your life *Very astute play since slogan is a half-anagram of company name: the "y" and "l" of Mylan are used to start the two words of the slogan*
Neuro [creams]	It's all about you

Nicorette	1) You can do it. Nicorette can help
	2) Makes quitting suck less
	3) For every cigarette there's a Nicorette
Optegra	Expert eye care
Optrex	We understand the language of eyes
	Not bad, were it not for the word "language" which would have been more appropriate for a medicine for the mouth
Orajel	Real relief in real time
Oral B Pro Expert [toothpaste]	The toothpaste our brushes have been waiting for
Oralyte	Hydrate right with Oralyte
	A timid attempt at a rhyme
Panadol	Body FIRST
Pearl Drops	For a whiter, brighter smile
Perfectil	The science of beauty
Pfizer	Life is our life's work
	Better than the older slogan "we are part of the cure"
Piri	Act before you React
Plan B	Because the unexpected happens*
	A remarkably simple slogan for a highly emotional event
Playtex Products [tampons]	Because comfort counts
Prozac (Eli Lilly)	Welcome back**
	Like the UPS motto, this one is very personal, maybe slightly indelicate, but a beautiful find
Rembrandt	1) Oral health and beauty
	2) Be your brightest

Right Guard	Keep your cool
Sea-Bond	Holds dentures, protects gums
Senokot Comfort	Feel happy inside
Seven Seas Jointcare	A spring in your step
Sominex	Count on us to help you drift off
Sudafed	Stops sinus pain before it starts
Superdrug.com	Take another look *Nice double play on investigating the product together with looking better*
Suremen [deodorant]	It won't let you down
Tampax	1) The one. The only. Tampax. 2) Outsmart Mother Nature* *Imaginative and lovely, for a particularly difficult brand*
Tylenol	Take comfort in our strength
Ultralase	Gold standard eye correction
Vagisil	The relief you need . . . right where you need it *A pretty good slogan for a very difficult subject*
Veet [cream]	1) Sensationally smooth 2) What beauty feels like
Viactiv	Active nutrition for women by women *Somewhat feminist*
Viagra	Ask your doctor. See the difference *They apparently resisted the temptation to replace "See" with "Feel", a bit daring but better*
Vicks	Breathe life in
Visx	The power to see
Vitabiotics	Where Nature meets Science

Vivarin	Making the most of every day
Voltarol	The joy of movement *Interesting play in which the very end result of the medicine is emphasised; note that the word "joy" is positioned slightly above the others*
Walgreens	1) The Pharmacy America trusts 2) Fast. Friendly. Flexible
Wellbox	How well do you want to live?
Wilkinson Sword	Free your skin
Willowbrook	Risers. Recliners
Zeno	Clearly outsmarts pimples *The "clearly" is unnecessary*
Zocor	It's your future. Be there

PHOTOGRAPHY

Canon	1) You and Canon can *This is a good try at a pun; but it tries just a bit too hard* 1a) You can* *This shortened version is much better* 2) From mind to matter 3) Know how *The latest is the best* 4) *image*ANYWARE ["i" in different colour] 5) Take more than pictures. Take stories
Fuji FinePix	Don't take photos. Take FinePix
Fujifilm	You can see the future from here
Kodak	Take pictures. Further *Try to memorise this slogan, and see how difficult it is to memorise the last word*

Konica Minolta	1) Do something important
	2) Only from the mind of Minolta
Kyocera	Products for a clear future
Leica	1) Fascination and precision
	2) My point of view*
	Uses the two different meanings of the word "view" well
Nikon	1) Step ahead
	Short and strong; a bit vague as to the type of company – why not a shoe-maker?
	2) At the heart of the image
	They could have continued in the same vein and used "Zoom ahead"
Olympus	Focus on life
Pentax	Aren't your pictures worth a Pentax?
	A rare interrogative form
Polaroid	See what develops
	Double use of word "develops", but not outstanding
Swarovski Optik	The world in your eyes
Walgreens	Where America takes its pictures
Zeiss [lenses]	We'll see you right

PRINTING EQUIPMENT

AlphaGraphics	Printshops of the future
Brother	At your side

PUBLISHING [SEE ALSO "MEDIA"]

Broadway Books	Available wherever books are sold
Crimson Publishing	Passionate about publishing.
DK	Where learning comes to life

Expert Books *The Garden to Kitchen Expert*	You grew it . . . now cook it
Houghton Mifflin	Independent publishers since 1832
Ian Allan	Britain's Leading Specialist Publisher
Lonely Planet [guide books]	The world awaits . . .
Plenum Publishing	The language of science
Vogue.com	The first look. The final word
Wiley-VCH	The new global force in scientific publishing

REAL ESTATE

Barnes Homes	International Property Consultant
Barrett Homes	1) Built around you *Underlines the fact that the owner has the priority in choices* 2) Find the one
Bective Leslie Marsh	Find out what you need, when you need it most
Countryside Properties [UK]	Thinking beyond today *The slogan in itself is good – but it contains nothing specific to real estate*
Crayson	Specialists in selling
Cushman & Wakefield	See beyond the expected
Douglas and Gordon	It doesn't hurt to know
Henry & James	Qualities

Jackson-Stops & Staff	Times change, but standards endure
Janine Stone	Creating exceptional homes for exceptional people
John D Wood & Co	Estate of mind agents *A pun on "a state of mind"*
Kinleigh Folkard & Hayward	Completely London
Knight Frank	Recipes for success
Marsh & Parsons	Local know how. Better results
Mountgrange Heritage	. . . values that you'll love
Oakwrights	Beautiful homes, uniquely crafted
Octagon	Bespoke
Primelocation.com	1) The more refined property search 2) The prime property website
RealEstate.com	The easiest part of getting a home
Regal Homes	Prepare to be inspired *Not sure whether this is a slogan, but it should be because it's good. Compare with Siemens in "Internet, Networks"*
Rightmove	Britain moves at Rightmove
WA Ellis	1) Quietly outstanding 2) Expect the best
Winkworth.co.uk	For thousands of properties to buy or rent
The World [ship]	The ultimate address** *Gets to the point really well*
Zoopla.co.uk	Smarter property search

RETAIL

Amazon.com	1) Earth's biggest selection 2) And you're done 3) A bookstore too big for the physical world
Argos	Find it. Get it. Argos it.
ASDA	Saving you money every day
Barnes & Noble	1) Booksellers since 1873 2) If we don't have your book, nobody does
Best Buy	Turn on the fun
Comet.co.uk	Come and play
Costcutter	Proud to be local
Dillard's	The style of your life
DSM	Bright Science. Brighter Living
Hawkin's Bazaar	Because life's too serious
House of Fraser	Since 1849
JC Penney	1) It's all inside 2) Every day matters
John Lewis Partnership	1) Never knowingly undersold *Although the store is true to its slogan, the motto itself is clumsy; actually, they have recently added a line "on quality/on price/on service"* 2) A lifelong commitment to quality
K-Mart	Compare and save at Super K-Mart
Lyoness	Together we are strong!
Macy's	The magic of Macy's

Pier Import	Get in touch with your senses *Compare with Baileys (p49)*
Primark	Amazing fashion. Amazing prices.
Sainsbury's	1) Try something new today 2) Live well for less *Better*
Target	Expect more. Pay less* *Uses "more" and "less" in a smart way*
TK Maxx	Big labels, small prices
Very.co.uk	The new online department store
Walmart	Always low prices
Waterstone's	Feel every word* *Rather good – with three words they manage to give a field-specific motto which speaks for itself*
WHSmith	Game on. Think WHSmith *Has a dot above the "m" and "i"*
Winn-Dixie	The real deal* *Nice rhyme*

SAILING

Arkin Pruva Yachts [Turkey]	Refined sailing for those wanting to enjoy the future whilst honouring the past
b-Yachts	Sail the difference
Camper & Nicholsons	Yachting since 1782 *Compare with many of the watchmaker slogans*
Ferretti Yachts	Created to seduce
Frers	Naval architecture and engineering
Furuno NavNet	Get some backbone . . .

Future Fibres	Tomorrow's innovation
Harken	Innovative sailing solutions
J Boats J-111	Better Sailboats for People Who Love Sailing
Latitude Yachts	Classic Yachts Construction
Navimo	On board with you
McMurdo	Safety for professionals
McMurdo Fast Find [search and rescue navigation]	Get found with Fast Find
The Moorings	Yacht ownership
mtu [yachts]	Power. Passion. Partnership *The third word is superfluous*
NorthSails [yachts]	Better by Design
Oyster Yachts	Even at sea level you can feel on top of the world* *Nicely put, using the physical "sea level" and the psychological "top of the world"*
Sandeman Yacht Company	Classic Yacht Brokers
Sevenstar Yacht Transport	A sea of choice . . . Oceans of experience *Like the Oyster slogan, a good play on the figurative meaning of the words in the slogan*
Southerly (Dubois Naval Architects)	World Leading Variable Draft Cruising Yachts
Stripper [propellor protector]	The bare essential for your propellor *The nude mermaid in the ad emphasises perfectly the "bare" word*

X-Yachts	World Class since 1979
Zeus (B&G)	The only chartplotter designed for sailing

SEMICONDUCTORS

Applied Materials	The information age starts here
Infineon Technologies	Never stop thinking

SOFTWARE [SEE ALSO "COMPUTING"]

Accenture [consulting]	1) Innovation delivered 2) High performance. Delivered
Adobe	Better by Adobe
Business Objects (SAP)	Business intelligence. If you have it, you know
Cap gemini	Ideas. People. Technology
CDW	1) Computing Solutions built for business 2) The right technology. Right away
Computer Associates	1) Software superior by design 2) The software that manages e-business
Compuware	1) People and software for business applications 2) What do you need most?
EMC²	Where information lives
E.S.Q	Software tools to manage your business

Hypercube Inc	The best chemistry
Hyperion	Listen to your business
JD Edwards	1) Run with it
	2) Software for a changing world
Lotus (IBM)	Working together
Microsoft	1) Where do you want to go today?
	The larger "you" has disappeared; for Microsoft, I would have expected a slogan with the word "soft" in it
	2) Software for the Agile business
	Hum...
	3) Your potential, our passion
	4) people "T" ready
	The "T" is actually a figure of a woman
	5) [Windows 7] The collection designed for individuals
Oracle	Unbreakable
PeopleSoft	1) Applications for e-business
	2) Past; Present; Future
	The brand name comes below the slogan
SAP	1) More than no-one in the world
	2) Certified business solutions
	3) The best-run businesses run SAP [changed to "The best-run companies run SAP"]
SAS	The power to know
Syntegra	The brains behind the scene
Veritas	Kiss your data hello*
	Highly imaginative

SPORTS

Adidas Adizero	Light makes fast
Altura	Technical bikewear

America's Olympic Team   Who's our next hero?

Asics   Sound mind, sound body

Aspire Qatar Academy   Aspire today, inspire tomorrow
[sports academy]

Assos   Sponsor yourself

Babolat   1) Tennis runs in our blood
Nice
2) Ultimate tennis experience

Bamboo [surfboards]   Laminate Technology

Cabrinha [kitesurfing]   Intelligent Depower System

Club Hotel Olivi   Where tennis is a lifestyle

Colnago [bikes]   True to Colnago
Rather self-satisfying

Cortez Surfboards   Epoxy Flight

Cycle Claims   The specialist firm for cycle
accidents

Dawes Cycles   Discover your world

Dunlop Sport   Quality products at quality prices

FC Barcelona   More than a club

FIFA   For the good of the game

Forme   Embracing the best of British
design

Genetrix [kites]   Wired instinct

Giordana   True passion for cycling

GNC   Live well

IKO Centers   It's a great feeling

Jack Wolfskin   For those who feel at home outdoors

Karakal [rackets]	Evolution by design
Kilo To Go	On your bike, Britain
Nobile Kiteboarding	Beyond expectations
O'Neill Hyperfleece	Stay out longer
Ozone C4	The future defined
Patagonia	1) Built for purpose *Nice* 2) Build the best products, cause no unnecessary harm, use business to inspire and implement solutions to the environmental crisis
Ping	Play your best
Purely Tennis	Where service matters . . . *Great play on the word "service"*
PWP	Europe's biggest Racketsport Specialist
Ribble Cycles	Established 1897
Salomon [skis]	Fuel your instinct
Sandown Park [racecourse]	Nowhere else comes close *Nice double meaning of "close", also implying the race itself*
Selle Italia	Saddles for winners since 1897
Shinn	All skills need practice
Surftech	Building boards for people who surf!
Takoon Kiteboarding	Suits all styles
Tipi Adventure	Learn it, live it, love it! *Quite a few recent slogans have adopted this triple interjection form; see for instance Whole Foods and MonaVie*
Vans Surf	Classic style. Modern comfort

Vision Kites	Superior versatility, exceptionally balanced
Weldtite	Fix it. Ride it
Wheelbase	UK's largest cycle store
Wilson	Number 1 in Tennis

TOBACCO

Camel	What you're looking for
Cifuentes [cigars]	An escape from the ordinary
Cohiba	A world beyond other cigars
Colibri [lighters]	Light years ahead
De Heeren van Ruysdael	The cigar of kings. And those who live like them
Havana Reserve	Unlimited pleasure, without reservations *Clearly redundant; the first two words would have sufficed – in spite of the attempt at recalling "reserve" with "reservation"*
Macanudo	An American passion
McClelland [pipe tobacco]	Take the time to enjoy the taste . . .
Parliament (Philip Morris)	1) The perfect recess 2) Distinctly smooth
Philip Morris Companies	Supporting the spirit of innovation
RJ Reynolds	1) Over 18,000 people in 170 countries *One of the very rare slogans to have numbers in it. See Four Seasons* 2) The key to success. People
Zino Davidoff [cigars]	A man, a cigar, a legend
Zippo	It works or we fix it free

TOURISM [SEE ALSO "HOTELS, RESORTS" AND "TRAVEL"]

Abu Dhabi	1) Travellers welcome 2) The world. Closer via Abu Dhabi
Andalucia	There's only one
Armenia	Noah's route. Your route* *Excellent. It wasn't easy to find a slogan for such a remote country*
Aspen	Renew
Australia	There's nothing like Australia
Austria	1) It's got to be Austria 2) Think Spa. Think Austria
Azerbaijan	Land of fire
Azores	Feel alive *Remarkably good for a group of islands*
Bahamas	It just keeps getting better
Barbados	Long Live *Life*
Barcelona	Experience Barcelona
Belgium	A state of mind *The accompanying TV ad, repeating "be" this or that, is outstanding*
Bermuda	Feel the love
Botswana	Redefining safari
Brazil	Sensational!
British Columbia	Super, Natural British Columbia
British Virgin Islands	Nature's little secrets
Bulgaria	Magic lives here *The French translation "la magie commence ici" (ie the magic starts here) seems better*

California	Find yourself here
Canada	Keep exploring
Cayman Islands	It's not who you know. It's where you know *Too bad it's so lengthy*
Chesapeake	Where business comes to life
Croatia	1) The Mediterranean as it once was 2) Sounds good
Cumbria	Britain's Energy Coast
Cyprus	1) The island for all seasons 2) In your heart
Denmark	Feel free *Not bad*
Dominican Republic	1) A land of sensations 2) Has it all
Dubai	1) Freedom to do business [Jebel Ali Free Zone] 2) The Centre of now [Downtown Dubai] 3) Definitely Dubai *Nice alliteration*
Egypt	1) Where everyone wears a smile 2) Where it all begins *An interesting reference to the past*
Georgia	Grow with Georgia
Greece	1) Experience life 2) Beyond words 3) Explore your senses
Greenland	Be a pioneer* *A great remembrance of the past and a good appeal for the future*

Grenada	The spice of the Caribbean
Guernsey	Not long haul, but miles away*
	Good way of saying that you can easily have the feeling of being far from home, even at a short distance – but the mileage here refers to the change of scenery
Hong Kong	1) Live it. Love it!**
	Lovely. Surprising nobody had ever thought of such a slogan for a touristic spot
	2) Asia's world city
	This far inferior slogan seems to have been chosen for the occasion of the WTO 6th Ministerial meeting
Hungary	Take a turn
Iceland	Discover the world
Illinois	A million miles from Monday
Incheon	The winged city
India	Incredible! India [with red dot under the exclamation mark]
	Nice rhyme
Indonesia	1) The world of its own
	2) Remarkable Indonesia
Iowa	The smart state for business
Ireland	1) Awaken to a different world
	2) Go where Ireland takes you
Israel	Tranquil oasis
Istria	Green Mediterranean
Italy	Much more
	Rather good, were it not that this slogan refers in no manner whatsoever to a country
Jersey	Turbo charge your weekend
Kenya	1) Discover the magic of Africa
	2) Magical
	Great for a single-word slogan

Louisiana	Come as you are. *Leave different*
Malaysia	Truly Asia *A very easy one to remember, because of the perfect rhyme*
Maldives	The sunny side of life
Malta	1) A stone's throw 2) Truly Mediterranean
Marrakech	Travel for real
Marseille Provence	You'll be moved!
Mauritius	Simply divine* *In a field where original slogans are hard to come by, a superb and simple slogan*
Mexico	1) Beyond your expectations 2) The place you thought you knew
Miami	Where worlds meet
Montenegro	Wild beauty
Morocco	1) Travel to a land of wonders 2) Travel for real
Namibia	Endless horizons
New Zealand	Simply remarkable
Nigeria	Good people. Great nation
Oman	Beauty has an address, Oman
Ontario	1) The future's right here 2) The world works here *Note how the slogan has been modified to attract people rather than investors*
Orlando	You never outgrow it
Pahang (Sultanate)	Nature's undiscovered gift

Peru	Live the legend
Portugal	1) Europe's West Coast
	The Portuguese, who are rightly proud of their country, could have found a better slogan, although on second thoughts it may serve its purpose and bring tourists in
	2) The beauty of simplicity
	Not much better because it could apply to nearly any company
Qatar	Once seen, never forgotten
Quebec	1) Closer than you think
	2) Providing emotions since 1534*
	An unusual historical perspective which gives the province a head start
Queensland	Where Australia shines
	The "Q" of Queensland has rays around it like sun-rays
Reynolds Mountain	Distinctly above it all*
	Nicely put, since it's a take on mountain height
St Lucia	Live the legend
Scotland	1) Best small country in the world
	2) Welcome to Scotland
	Deservedly criticised since it says nothing about the country
	3) Surprise yourself
Sicily	1) Everything else is in the shade
	2) Myth into an island of light
Singapore	So easy to enjoy. So hard to forget**
	Very poetic
South Africa	It's possible
Spain	Lost at last!*
	Lovely
Switzerland	Switzerland. Naturally
	Somewhat pretentious

Syria	Land of civilisations
Thailand	1) A beautiful reason to smile
	2) Exceed your expectations*
	Excellent, with repeat of the "ex ..."
Tunisia	The future is here today
Turkey	1) Fascinates
	2) Welcomes you
	These two slogans have quite a different emphasis
Virginia	Virginia is for lovers
Wales	For proper holidays

TOYS AND GAMES [SEE ALSO "RETAIL"]

Bingo	Put some play in your day
EA Games	Challenge everything
EA Sports	It's in the game
Fisher-Price	Oh, the possibilities!
	Rare use of the exclamation mark
PlayStation	1) Live in your world. Play in ours
	Rather nice; makes us think what it's all about
	2) Your turn
	Better
Tidlo	Timeless toys
Toys R Us	Only at Toys R Us [R often written backwards with a star inside the top, circular part of the letter]
Xbox	1) Play more
	2) Jump in
	Beautifully short – but to anybody who wouldn't know what this slogan refers to, somewhat meaningless

135

TRAVEL [SEE ALSO "TOURISM" AND "HOTELS, RESORTS"]

Airtours (Thomas Cook)	The holiday makers
Alstom	We are shaping the future
Amazon Creek	Ultimate Luxury Holidays
Amtrak	Now arriving
Anahita	Live in your dream
Blue Water Holidays	The UK's only specialists in holidays afloat
Bombardier ZEFIRO	The fastest way to save the planet
Brittany Ferries	Where holidays begin
Caribbean Connection	Luxury travel is our speciality
Celebrity Cruises	Exceeding expectations
Crystal Cruises	1) The most glorious ships at sea 2) The difference is Crystal clear* *Very nice*
Cunard	Where else in the world
DeltaRail	Software and Technology for the rail industry
ESG	Designed to deliver
Eurostar	Opening the way
Executive Jet	Judge a company by the customers it keeps
Expedia.co.uk	We're powered by people who travel
First Great Western	Putting you first
Fodor's	An adventure on every page

Haven	Britain's favourite seaside holiday
Hayes & Jarvis	Unmistakable value
Holland America Line	A signature of excellence
Hotels.com	Wake up happy
Hotwire.com	4-star hotels, 2-star prices
Invensys Rail	A more powerful solution across the board
Kirker	For discerning travellers
Kuoni	No one knows the planet like us
Lowcostholidays.com	Now anyone can go anywhere
MSC Cruises	The most modern fleet in the world
National Rail	Life begins off-peak
Norwegian Cruise Line	Freestyle cruising
Oceania Cruises	Your world. Your way
Orient Lines	The destination cruise specialists
P&O Cruises	There's a world out there
P&O Ferries	Expect more
Page & Moy	Immerse yourself
Powder Byrne	The luxury holiday company for parents and kids
Princess Cruises	Escape completely
Ramblers	Worldwide Holidays
Regent Seven Seas Cruises	Luxury goes exploring
Royal Caribbean Cruises	Get out there

Samsonite	1) Our strengths are legendary
	2) Worldproof
	Much better than the previous one, since it implies, in a single word, the function of the company
Scenic Tours	The ultimate touring experience
Seabourn [cruises]	When only the best will do
Silversea	1) One aim, one excellence
	2) Explore. Dream. Discover
Surreal Holidays	Beyond your imagination
	I would have preferred a slogan picking up on "surreal": real holiday, surreal living
Thomas Cook	Don't just book it. Thomas Cook it.
	Nice – plus the rhyme
Thomson	Your holiday to a T
Transys Projects Limited	Assured Rail Vehicle Solutions
Travel Channel	Be a traveller
Traveler	1) Why be a tourist when you can be a traveler?
	2) Truth in travel
	3) Holidays created by the people who know
Traveler's Insider's Guide	The last trip you'll ever take without leaving home
Travelex.com	Before you travel, Travelex
Trip.com	Simply brilliant
	A good slogan, but it doesn't tell us why this company should be chosen over others
Viking River Cruises	Exploring the world in comfort
Virgin Holidays	Ask for the world

Voyageprivé.com   Dream travel within reach. For members only

Wildlife & Culture Holidays   Immerse yourself*
The slogan does let your imagination go wild

WEDDINGS

Casablanca Bridal   Celebrate forever
Nicely put

Crate & Barrel   The wedding parties

David's Bridal   Get inspired

Gray & Farrar   The ultimate matchmaking service

Kate Aspen   Unforgettable Favors

Michaels [weddings]   Where creativity happens

Oleg Cassini   Fashionable. Affordable. Unforgettable

Sandals   Luxary Included Vacations

Watters   Dream designs for dream weddings

Wedding Paper   Simply perfect, perfectly simple
Compare with Patrón Tequila

MISCELLANEOUS

AdSlogans   1) It pays to check
2) Where the endline comes first
Though the second one is more amusing, I prefer the first one

Bonhams   Since 1793

Boys and Girls Clubs of America	The positive place for kids
Care Village Group	It's all about you
Churchill War Rooms	The rooms that changed history
Council for Biotechnology Information	Good ideas are growing
Dreweatts & Bloomsbury	Working together
Duke's	If you are thinking of selling, think Duke's
Hoover Institution	Ideas defining a free society
IAA (International Advertising Association)	Advertising. The right to choose
Indesit	We work, you play
Manpower	Here and now
Thorpe	Spill out

PART 2
SLOGAN STORIES

AA (AUTOMOBILE ASSOCIATION)

Although the AA was created in 1905 with an objective which now seems outdated – avoiding police speed traps – it has now become an association which essentially helps motorists. First of all, it gives roadside assistance, with a 24-hour breakdown and recovery service. But it also provides insurance to motorists and has become the UK's largest motor insurance company. Last but not least, it provides excellent driving lessons at a reasonable cost, for members and non-members alike. Its headquarters are in Basingstoke. AA, together with the insurance and travel company Saga Group, forms part of Acromas Holdings Ltd whose CEO is Andrew Goodsell.

In their old village signs the AA used the slogan **"safety first"**. But the official slogan is now **"For the road ahead"**. It is accompanied by a short film starting with "The AA has more dedicated patrols than any other UK breakdown service . . .". The slogan was introduced very recently (March 2009) by the MBA Agency (London), whose Chief Executive is Stephen Maher. According to the agency, the introduction of the slogan contributed to a 66% increase in response, ie the number of people who take out breakdown cover. Their creative publicity also played a role, and the percentage of increase has still to be tested on a larger cross-section of the population. In a lovely short 21-second TV ad (June 2010) you see a fleet of yellow AA vans rushing out of their garage. One of them arrives at a broken-down car – and immediately the AA man repairs the problem. He and the thankful driver shake hands, and he's off. The tagline is "If you're not already a member of the world's largest motoring association, join AA now. It's great to belong." The music is Rimski Korsakov's "Flight of the Bumble Bee", which emphasises the speed at which the work is done.

ABERCROMBIE AND FITCH

Founded in 1892 in Manhattan by David Abercrombie and Ezra Fitch, the company now has its headquarters in New Albany, Ohio. When one walks into the London Abercrombie and Fitch

(A & F) store (formally on 42 Savile Row, but the main entrance is at 7 Burlington Gardens), one gets a shock. You are greeted by ultra-loud music, a throng of potential client youngsters, a half-naked male model at the entrance (apparently there are two who alternate all day), dozens of A & F sales assistants, easily recognisable and very helpful, and, last but not least, gigantically high cases with innumerable shelves of A & F sweaters. There are no black sweaters (A & F is dedicated to happiness) but there are some very dark navy-blue sweaters . . . Two enormous cupboards contain memorabilia such as skis, reminding us that the company has ties to the Adirondacks as a sporting goods company (in 1939 they considered themselves the greatest in the world), and rifles – telling us that Hemingway may have bought his gun at A & F. The size of A & F can be measured by the fact that two of its subsidiaries, Hollister (South California) and Gilly Hicks (Australia) also have a good measure of success.

The A & F logo is a moose, which can be found on all its clothes. Hollister has its own logo – a flying seagull. The A & F slogan, **"Casual Luxury"**, seems to date back to 2005, after the opening of the flagship store on Fifth Avenue, and originated with in-house Marketing Director Mark Jeffries. It implies that A & F clothing is high-end (cashmere, pima cotton, etc) but can still be worn daily. CEO since 1992, Michael Jeffries can be credited for turning A & F around from a mere sporting-goods company into one dedicated to youth and fun.

ADIDAS

Adidas is a German-based sports apparel company which essentially sells sports-shoes, with an emphasis on tennis and football. It derives from the Dassler Brothers Shoe Factory, founded by Adi and Rudolf Dassler in 1924. The brothers split up after the Second World War with Adidas AG being registered on 18 August 1949 by Adi Dassler, whose first six letters are easily recognisable in the brand name. After several twists and turns, including one involving French businessman Bernard Tapie, and the purchase of French skiwear Salomon Group plus British rival Reebok, Adidas is again an independent company, headquartered in Herzogenaurach, Bavaria, Germany. Its CEO is Herbert Hainer and the Chairman of the Board is Igor Landau.

The major Adidas slogan is **"Impossible is nothing"** (ad agency 180/TBWA Amsterdam; Executive Director Alex Joseph; see also AXA article on page 148). It dates back to May–June 2006 and the 2006 Football World Cup for which Adidas was one of the official sponsors (and again in 2010). In a lovely 1 minute 1 second ad accompanying this slogan (production company Stink Ltd, London), one sees two 10-year-old boys on a cement playground in a poor neighbourhood. "José, vamos?" asks one boy. "Si", answers the other. In turn they start calling out the names of their players – and an extraordinary event happens. As the boys call out famous soccer players – "Cissé, Kaka, Zidane, Beckham, Jermain Defoe, Oliver Kahn, Messi . . ." those players actually appear on the playing field! One boy then calls out, "Beckenbauer!" The other child laughs at him, "Beckenbauer", as if it was a ridiculous possibility, like calling God Himself. But Beckenbauer does appear, and even Oliver Kahn can't believe his eyes. So the other child is envious, and Zidane whispers to him "Platini!". So the child calls Platini and – lo and behold! – Platini arrives also. The last two players appear as they were in their prime. The game starts and the **"Impossible is nothing"** slogan appears.

AMAZON.COM

When one talks about the great internet success stories of the last decade, one immediately thinks of Amazon. The Amazon.com company was founded in 1994 by Jeff Bezos, its present President, CEO and Chairman of the Board. In 17 years the number of employees has grown to some 34,000. The company originally focused on selling books online though it has now diversified into DVDs, video games, toys, shoes, kitchen equipment, furnishings, etc. It is headquartered in Seattle. Whereas the original logo was a large capital A letter with a long river crossing through it and seen in perspective (see *www.kokogiak.com/gedankengang/2004/07/ amazoncom-logo-timeline.html*), the present logo is simply the company name with an underscore curved arrow linking the "a" of "Amazon" to the "z".

Early slogans (1995) for Amazon.com were **"The world's largest bookstore"** or the variant **"The earth's biggest bookstore"**. However, in 2002 the company introduced the slogan **". . . and you're done"**. I have yet to see videos featuring either slogan. However, there are numerous videos boasting Amazon's "Kindle" the company's own e-reader. Some ads have apparently been aimed against Apple's iPad (see below), but other ads insist on the compatibility between the Kindle and its competitors. One good 33-second Kindle ad (September 2010) shows a large pool lined with palm trees. A young lady is reading from a Kindle as she relaxes on a mattress. A fellow besides her (apparently holding an iPad) says: "Excuse me. How are you reading that? In this light?". She answers, "It's a Kindle. 139 dollars. I actually paid more for these sunglasses!" And the ad ends with **"The all-new Kindle"**. Another TV ad boasts 800,000 books and claims that the Kindle is "lighter than a paperback". Although the ad concludes in a book-friendly manner ("The book lives on!"), it is clear that this ad highlights the ongoing feud between Amazon and "physical" bookstores. Personally I prefer to read a "physical" book, but on the other hand I have greatly profited from being able to order books from Amazon which can not be found anywhere else.

AMERICAN AIRLINES

American Airlines, the world's third largest airline by scheduled passengers carried (105 million in 2010) and first by passengers multiplied by kilometres flown (197 billion), is headquartered in Fort Worth, Texas. The Chairman of the Board and CEO is Gerard Arpey.

An American Airlines plane (a Boeing 767, flight 11 from Boston to Los Angeles) was involved in the first of the two 9/11 attacks on the Twin Towers and crashed into the North Tower at 8.45am on that fateful day. A second flight (flight 77 from Washington to LA, a Boeing 757) crashed into the Pentagon at 9.43am. Right after 9/11, American Airlines initiated a TV ad campaign with the words: "We are an airline, but it's become clear we are more. We are a way of life, the freedom to come and go, anywhere, anytime, with confidence and peace of mind. We are an airline that's proud to bear the name . . . American!" with a slightly nationalistic overtone at the end.

In September 2004 the AA ad agency TM Advertising (part of the Interpublic Group), which held the AA account since 1981, introduced the **"We know why you fly"** slogan, replacing the 1984–2000 slogan **"Something special in the air"** (before that, there was **"the ontime machine"**). The key executives in the account were Group Creative Director Bill Oakley, Creative Director Shep Kellam, Copywriter Jason Niebaum, Art Director Chris Cima and Producer Hal Dantzler (production Moxie Pictures). One short (30 sec) TV ad (1 October 2006) starts with an AA plane descending into the clouds. A stewardess announces the landing (probably in Chicago) of this AA flight coming in from Tokyo after an all-night trip. Then the camera points at a passenger still happily sleeping, with a faint smile on his face, while you can still hear the stewardess announcing all the possible flight connections. The slogan follows with the tagline **"American Airlines flies to Shanghai, Tokyo and Delhi every day"**.

AUSTRALIA

Australia is a continent in its own right, the discovery of which dates back to 1606 by the Dutch navigator Willem Janszoon. Although it is an independent country, Australia still maintains ties to the United Kingdom, thanks to a Governor-General representing the Queen. The present Prime Minister is Julia Gillard, and the total population is more than 22 million. The Australian flag requires a bit of deciphering: in addition to the Union flag on the upper left, there lies below it the Commonwealth Star representing the six Australian States and the Territories. On the right there are four largish stars representing the Southern Cross constellation (they are labelled Alpha, Beta, Gamma and Delta as in the Greek alphabet), plus a smaller "Epsilon" star which is actually only 57 light years away from the Earth.

The current slogan promoting Australia is **"There's nothing like Australia"**, which was launched by DDB Sydney on 31 March 2010. The slogan was quickly followed by a series of TV ads, one of which – at 1 minute 30 seconds, directed by Michael Gracey, with Prodigy Films as production company and music by Josh Abrahams – shows a series of typical Australian images. It starts off with two surfers at sunset, with some dolphins in the distance: "There's nothing like it, is it? There's nothing like the sunrise, the first wave of the day . . . The trip along the coastline . . . " Here, as further down, each verse is accompanied by a new shot – some of which are striking: a piano on the beach at dawn, sunset on camels also along a beach, a girl holding a koala, a herd of kangaroos, and of course the Sydney Opera House with fireworks . . . The only issue was that the city of Wellington, New Zealand independently and at exactly the same time, launched the slogan **"There's no place like Wellington"**, aimed at . . . Australian tourists!

AXA

AXA S.A. is the ninth largest company in the world, with a revenue of 91 billion euros in 2010. The original insurance company was founded in Marseilles in 1816. It acquired the name AXA in 1985 under its then Chairman Claude Bébéar. Its present Chairman and CEO is Henri de Castries. AXA is involved in "basic" insurance (car, travel, home), medical insurance, life insurance, reinsurance (ie insuring other smaller insurance companies) and also asset management. Its headquarters are in Paris.

The **"be life confident"** slogan was created in 2003 by TBWA agency (founded in 1970 by William G. Tragos [American], Claude Bonnange [French], Ull Wiesendanger [Swiss], Paolo Ajroldi [Italian]). The slogan is meant to imply that confidence in AXA leads to a better life. But the word "life" has been criticised by some (John Morrish, *Management Today,* 8 April 2005). A short (32 seconds) recent video shows a female AXA employee who boasts the merits of AXA insurance and says, "It's a very personal thing, because you get to know people and you develop a personal relationship with them. . . .". "AXA and you, perfect together", says the ad commentator. The more recent slogan, **"Redefining standards"** is owing to an in-house "Brand Spirit" branding task force. A very intriguing 1 minute 44 seconds ad has *no* images – it just runs through a series of sentences, from top to bottom, and then backwards from bottom to top. The first reading can be summarised by "People are sceptical about AXA" while the second reading on the contrary says that "People can be confident with AXA". Simply the "verses" are cut in a different way. What reads downwards as "We work in an industry where promises are not kept . . . So customers will never believe that . . . We have their interests at heart . . . Our customers must think that. . . ." becomes, upwards, "Our customers must think that . . . We have their interests at heart . . . So customers will never believe that . . . We work in an industry where promises are not kept . . .".

BAILEYS

Baileys, the world's bestselling liqueur, belongs to global alcoholic beverage company Diageo, headed by Franz Humer (Chairman) and Paul Walsh (CEO). Other Diageo brands are Guinness (see page 166), Johnnie Walker and Smirnoff. The process for manufacturing Baileys liqueur is quite complex: it uses whey, the liquid residue from milk after the removal of cheese curds during the manufacture of cheese, which is fermented. The whey is mixed with specific yeast strains and left to macerate for several days. After 72 hours, typical experiments show the alcohol content going from zero to more than 10% – Baileys has 17%. Next the alcohol is mixed with cream, with the help of an emulsifier. Thus, although honey, coffee and cocoa are also added, most of Baileys liqueur originates from . . . milk! The bottles have a nice shape; under the Baileys label it says, "The original Irish Cream".

Until 2008, Baileys grand slogan was **"Let your senses guide you"** (BBH London). A recent video on this theme features a man and a woman in a bar. They toast with Baileys. The woman spills some of hers – "sense of loss". The man wipes it off the table – "sense of duty". But right after this he also wipes a drop off the woman's dress, on her bosom – "sense of adventure". The Baileys slogan ends the video. In November 2008 the slogan **"Listen to your lips"** was introduced by JWT in London. A short video shows a multitude of women's lips aimed upwards as drops of Baileys fall into them. One last drop falls into the cocktail glass. Various still ads just show a woman's lips twisted in desire, with the Baileys slogan printed nearby – but it is difficult, for the layman looking at these stills, to surmise what the woman's desire is really directed at.

BARCLAYS

Barclays PLC is one of the leading British banks and also the world's tenth largest banking and financial services institution. Indeed, Barclays, like many important banks, has two different fields of thrust: retail banking for the layman, and more discrete service banking, ie investment banking (Barclays Capital), commercial banking (Barclays Corporate) and wealth management (Barclays Wealth). The Barclays logo, redrawn and recoloured in 1981, represents a Germanic spreadeagle[†] and dates back to 1690 when the founders set up a business in London; the name Barclays itself dates back to 1736 and uses the surname of James Barclay, son-in-law of one of the founders of the business (1690), who became a partner that year. Barclays, whose headquarters are located in Canary Wharf, sponsors the famed English football Premier League. The Barclays PLC Group Chief Executive is American banker Robert E. Diamond, Jr (since 1 January 2011).

A famous Barclays slogan, **"Fluent in Finance"**, was introduced in 2002 by Bartle Bogle Hegarty (BBH; Marc Hatfield and Pete Bradly), and roughly lasted for the decade. The most recent slogan, again due to BBH (Creative Directors Matt Doman, Ian Heartfield and Mark Reddy), is **"Take one small step"**. It was launched in March 2009, quite near the peak of the banking crisis (fourth quarter of 2008), which is possibly indicative of the measured nature of the slogan. Often the word "step" is displaced above the other three words of the slogan, so as to illustrate an actual

---

† In 2007, when Barclays was due to merge with ABN-AMRO, there had been talk of dropping the eagle logo; but the merger failed.

staircase step. The underlying idea is that Barclays makes your money bear fruit in simple controlled steps. The slogan was later used by MezzoFilms to promote an online £50,000 competition for Barclays clientele.

BBC

The BBC name covers a complex string of media institutions. Summarily, the BBC is a corporation headed by a Director General (newly appointed George Entwistle) and overseen by a board called the BBC Trust (Chairman, Lord Patten of Barnes). Founded on 18 October 1922, the BBC now has some 23,000 employees and earns 75% of its revenue from the annual television licence fee. In addition to its 10 national radio networks, the BBC has eight TV channels BBC1, BBC2, BBC3, BBC4, BBC News, BBC Parliament, CBBC and CBeebies – all freely accessible via Freeview. BBC World News is the BBC's international arm.

The BBC is possibly most famous and admired for the role of BBC Radio during World War Two (television broadcasting had been suspended as of 1 September 1939). On 13 May 1940 the BBC broadcast the memorable Commons speech of Churchill, "I have nothing to offer but blood, toil, tears and sweat [later shortened to "Blood, sweat and tears"] . . . Without victory there is no survival". On 18 June 1940 De Gaulle made his famous BBC 6pm appeal: "Whatever happens, the flame of the French resistance must not be extinguished, nor will it be so".

The BBC used the slogan **"A perfect day"** from at least 1997 to 2006. One famous 1997 TV spot had 29 different singers singing the 38 lines of Lou Reed's famous song. At the end of the film you see, "Whatever your musical taste . . . it is catered for by . . . BBC Radio and Television" and **"You make it what it is"**. This last sentence was actually used as an earlier slogan in the 1990s. On 25 March 2006 the slogan **"This is what we do"** was introduced by ad agency Fallon, with a first ad showing a BBC crew with World Affairs Editor John Simpson going into Kabul with 28 donkeys. The two slogans have noticeable similarities. At the time of writing, Simpson is currently courageously covering the events in Libya.

BMW

BMW are the initials for Bayerische Motoren Werke AG. The
company was founded in 1916 and its headquarters are in Munich.
BMW manufactures cars (since 1928) as well as motorcycles
(since 1923). It has also owned the car-manufacturing part of
Rolls-Royce since 1998/9. Before discussing the slogan I should
mention the logo, a circle cut into four quarters, alternating white
and light blue. It is not clear whether this logo has its origin as
symbolising a whizzing propeller – white blades cutting through a
blue sky – or as the flag of the former Kingdom of Bavaria, with a
background of alternating light blue and white lozenges.

The slogan **"The ultimate driving machine"** has been BMW's
since 1975, when it was introduced by advertisers Ralph Ammirati
(then 48 years old) and Martin Puris (aged 36) who had just
founded their advertising agency in New York. They had already
been successful with ads for Fiat. It would appear that Bob Lutz,
Executive Vice-President of Sales for three years at BMW (1972–4),
and a member of its board of management, was responsible for
choosing this agency. Although Mullen Advertising gained the
BMW account on 11 February 1993 at the expense of Ammirati and
Puris, the original slogan has never been abandoned and has
played an important role in the company's success. From time to
time there are rumours that the slogan is going to be changed, for
instance, in 2006, in favour of "A company of ideas" – but as
marketing professional Joey Babs points out on BMW Blog (4
November 2009) "when you drive a BMW you simply cannot deny
the fact that they make automobiles that are more than a point A to
a point B car, more than a means of transportation. There is a spirit
behind these cars, these are drivers' cars and are meant to be
enjoyed." An interesting 3 minute 14 second online internet ad
(November 2008) for the BMW 5 series[†] shows hundreds of bubbles
– seemingly oval in shape – floating around endlessly in space.
The words "Innovation . . . Technology . . . Design . . . [and then
switching to German] . . . Verantwortung (responsibility) . . .
Kompetenz (competence) . . . Mobilität (mobility) . . ." slowly appear

† Thank you to Steffen Vogel (BMW Group) for information on this ad.

and disappear at the back. And just when the onlooker is totally bored, the bubbles get together and form the outline of . . . a car!

BOOTS

Boots was founded in 1849 by John Boot as a herbal medicine shop. In October 2005 it merged with Alliance Unichem and was taken into private ownership. As of today it is the pharmaceutical, healthcare and beauty subsidiary of Alliance Boots GmBH, headquartered in Zug, Switzerland, and chaired by Italian-born Stefano Pessina. Boots extends its reach into the optical and photographic sectors.

The major Boots slogan was **"Trust Boots"** before it was replaced in 2008 by the new slogan **"Feel Good"** (developed jointly by a number of agencies led by Mother Ltd UK, Shoreditch and Boots in 2008)[t]. It is an abbreviation of sorts of the brand positioning "To champion everyone's right to feel good".[t] There have been some excellent TV ads illustrating these slogans. In November 2007, a 1 minute 3 second ad featured women in a huge office who are seen to start discreetly putting on make-up. Slowly the movement gains momentum, with bathrooms full of girls glamming up. In a separate room the men are totally disconcerted. Finally an enormous crowd of women marches out to the tune of "Here come the girls" sung by the Sugarbabes. A final sign says "It's the season to be . . . **Gorgeous**". The tagline **"Trust Boots"** ends the ad. In another Mother Ltd ad (November 2010, 30 seconds), called "Surprise", a Christmas party is being held. A female guest opens her presents. She says, "I think I know what it is". Disappointed, she asks, "It's fruits?" The host answers, "Well actually, that's not just any fruit. That's the fruit that you'll be taking to your jam, preserves and pickles course!" She looks crushed. Then he gives her a second present, "Only joking! Got you this Sanctuary sumptuous gift [referring to Sanctuary Spa]".[t] She's thrilled and kisses him. Then

---

t Thanks to Fiona Lakin, PR Manager at the Boots Press Office, and to Elizabeth Fagan, Marketing Director of Boots, for this information.

‡ Thank you to Alison Hemmings for this information.

the tagline "Get 3 for 2 on gifts you know women will love at Boots" followed by the slogan **"Feel Good"**.

BP

BP is a global petroleum exploration and service station company headquartered in London. Founded in 1909 as the Anglo-Persian Oil Company, BP's present name dates back to 1954. The Chairman of the Board (since 1 January 2010) is Carl-Henric Svanberg and the CEO (since 1 October 2010) is Robert Dudley. BP reached unfortunate worldwide fame with the "Deepwater Horizon" oil spill, which occurred on 20 April 2010 after a drilling rig blew up and sank in the Gulf of Mexico, killing 11 people. It took some three months to stop the flow of crude oil from one mile below the broken rig. The business and ecological damages to five US states (Florida, Louisiana, Alabama, Mississippi, Texas) were enormous and BP committed itself to a $20 billion spill response fund; as of 23 August 2011 a quarter of this had been paid out. Bob Hayward, CEO at the time of the spill, resigned after an all-out effort to stop the spill and after much apology.

An early BP slogan was **"On the move"** (Doner International ad agency) dating back to at least 1988. In 2000, Ogilvy and Mather (Creative Director David Fowler, Producer David Cohen) launched **"Beyond Petroleum"**, which remains BP's slogan today. At the same time BP changed its logo to a sunflower, albeit a rather special one with colours white, yellow and green from the inside out. One effective 38-second video comic strip (April 2007, Ogilvy & Mather New York) shows four tiny tots (the future generation of drivers!) in a car. They sing "Say hey! Make the day a little better! Say hey. . .". The car comes up to a BP gas station, where the fuel pumps start dancing too. Then comes the tagline "gas stations a little better, baby", followed by the sunflower and the BP slogan. The song was inspired by the "L.A." song from the band Message of the Blues. This strip is excellent for the happiness it conveys.

BRITISH AIRWAYS (BA)

British Airways is the flag carrier of the UK. Its headquarters are in Waterside, near its main hub at Heathrow. After forming the "one-world alliance" with American Airlines, Cathay Pacific and Qantas in February 1999, BA launched IAG, the "International Airlines Group", by merging with Iberia in January 2011. IAG is now the world's third largest airline. The CEO of British Airways is Keith Williams, and Martin Broughton is Chairman of the Board.

The slogan **"The World's Favourite Airline"** was introduced in 1989 by Saatchi and Saatchi, with a famous "Face" advertisement. The ad starts with swimmers, and goes on to make a human lip out of the swimmers gone ashore; then an ear appears; finally thousands of people together form a human face as seen from far above. The musical theme accompanying the slogan has always been the "Flower Duet" from Leo Delibes' opera Lakmé (1883; thus in 1989, just over 100 years after its creation, this opera was in the public domain). This has been rearranged for some ads, using "Aria on Air" by Malcolm McLaren, but the theme is still clearly recognised as Delibes' (see also www.secondhandsongs.com).

In 2004 a slogan **"The way to fly"** was introduced by Saatchi and Saatchi in another TV commercial, in which a fellow in New York takes a taxi to Kennedy; flies in a flat bed of the new Club World Class; and finally is reunited with his family in London. There is, of course, an orchestra playing the "Flower Duet", albeit . . . in the sea!

In 2009 BBH (Bartle, Bogle, Hegarty; creative director Mick Mahoney) introduced nine TV spots, 30 seconds each, with the purpose of inducing people to fly (the concept was "opportunity doesn't always live on your doorstep"). The first TV spot focused on the forthcoming Mumbai fashion week – and by doing so hoped to capitalise on the success of the *Slumdog Millionaire* movie – and the second on the migration of 2 million wildebeest in the Serengeti. Last but not least, on 21 September 2011, BA launched a new slogan **"To fly. To serve"** (BBH London again). A 90-second advert by Frédéric Planchon and Academy Films illustrates the new slogan.

BRITISH GAS

The status of British Gas has evolved over the years. Three successive Gas Acts (1948, 1972 and 1986) modelled the British Gas plc company, responsible up until February 1997 for domestic gas supply, service and installation and retail. Since 1997 further reorganisation has occurred and British Gas as we now know it really belongs to Centrica, a Windsor-based company chaired by Sir Roger Carr, with Sam Laidlaw as CEO. Centrica is a constituent of the FTSE 100 index. British Gas is now Europe's leading installer of central heating boilers and systems, offers energy-efficient boilers and designer radiators and, last but not least, supplies gas and electricity to many UK households. Interestingly, and seemingly without any specific reason for choosing this particular sport, British Gas sponsors British Swimming. A £15 million sponsorship deal was signed in March 2009 and announced by British Swimming Chief Executive David Sparkes and BG Marketing Director Rick Vlemmiks.

The ad company CHI & Partners (London) is responsible for the recent (2008–09) slogan **"Looking after your world"**, a collaboration via the "Big Ideas" process at CHI. Although one TV ad supporting this slogan was banned by the Advertising Standards Authority (28 April 2010 – because it gave the impression that it could carry out repairs even on Christmas day), another 31-second ad (March 2009) is charming. It shows a couple, living on their own planet, who make their home greener by throwing litter away, and then states: "We're [BG] doing our part" by "building the world's largest offshore wind farm" and by "providing you with renewable and affordable energy for the future". The video was created by Hornet Inc (New York) and directed by Guilherme Marcondes. Another nice 30-second spot (October 2010) shows a house turning upside down (originally with British Gas written upside down at the top) and states: "We know being without heating or hot water can turn your world upside down" (by CHI creatives Matt Pam and Simon Hipwell).[†]

Very recently British Gas has introduced the short **"Energy Smart"** method for reading meters and paying bills – but it could equally be used as a slogan, which may prove to be a success.

† Thank you to Adam Wintour at CHI for the slogan information.

CADBURY

Cadbury was founded in 1824 when John Cadbury opened a shop selling tea and chocolate drinks in Birmingham. It is interesting to note that during that same year Philippe Suchard started selling chocolate in Neuchatel, Switzerland. Cadbury's Dairy Milk bar was launched in 1905. Many Cadbury chocolate bars still bear this name. Cadbury (like Suchard) now belongs to Kraft Foods. When Kraft took over Cadbury, the chief executives of Cadbury resigned – the CEO of Kraft, Irene Rosenfeld, took over.

For a long time ads for a particular Cadbury chocolate bar were dedicated to the "Flake Girl". She might, for instance, be a lightly-dressed red-haired girl in a field of sunflowers, who climbs into her car and opens a Flake bar. A male voice pronounces **"The Crumbliest Flakiest milk chocolate in the world"**. Another sultry ad shows a woman (Rachel Brown) nibbling her Flake bar in a bathtub.

After the relative failure of the **"Your happiness loves Cadbury"** slogan in 2005, Publicis introduced the slogan **"A glass and a half full of joy"**. The most famous promotional ad for this slogan is the "Gorilla Drummer" ad, launched on 31 August 2007. The ad agency is Fallon London; the ad was directed by Argentina-born Juan Cabral and produced by Matthew Fore and Nicky Barnes, and the actor in a gorilla costume is Garon Michael, who had already played great-ape roles in movies. The ad lasts 1 minute 41 seconds. For the first 50 seconds we see just the gorilla's face, without having any idea of what it might be doing. After 1 minute, we see it drumming vigorously. In the last 5 seconds the Cadbury slogan appears, with milk pouring down from a glass and another half-glass, to make two chocolate cubes. The ad is accompanied by drummer Phil Collins' "In the Air Tonight". Although some people complained that a gorilla has nothing to do with chocolate, this commercial was a great success.

CHRISTIAN DIOR

For many a layman, the name "Dior" symbolises haute couture and luxury clothing. The Christian Dior company was founded on

16 December 1946 by clothing designer Christian Dior (then
41 years old) and textile magnate Marcel Boussac, famous for
his horse-racing stables. Their first fashion show took place on
12 February 1947 and brought instant fame to their company.
Boussac and Dior simultaneously launched a perfume company.
The Miss Dior perfume, created by Jean Carles and Paul Vacher, is
still a bestseller. In 1969 Bernard Arnault, owner of LVMH, united
the perfumes and clothing sectors as he bought a controlling stake
in Dior. Dior has now some 160 boutiques worldwide.

Two significant periods in the growth of Dior are the 1957–60 one
under Yves Saint Laurent and the 1997–2011 one under John
Galliano. Promoted to artistic director at the age of 21, Saint
Laurent had just time to create six fashion shows for Dior before
being dismissed in 1960. He went on to create his own fashion
company with the famous logo of intertwined Y, S and L letters.
Gibraltar-born John Galliano became creative director of Dior in
1997, and was a successful and emblematic figure there until he
was fired by Dior on 1 March 2011.

The **"J'adore Dior"** exclamation, which often accompanies
publicity for the perfume J'adore created in 1999 by master-
perfumer Calice Becker, is not considered by Dior to be a slogan,
but rather an expression linked to Dior's historical patrimony. A
very enticing 30-second TV ad for this perfume was run in April
2007 and shows Charlize Theron undressing completely as she
walks towards us through a series of rooms. It is all very proper but
very . . . sexy and still runs years later.

CISCO

Cisco was founded in 1984–5 by Len Bosack and Sandy Lerner
from Stanford University, and Richard Troiano. The name Cisco is
none other than the last two syllables of San Francisco. The
company essentially makes routers, ie devices which serve to
forward packages of information, in particular internet data. Each
home which receives or sends internet data must have either such
a router or a modem. Cisco has diversified in recent years, for
instance into cable TV products via the 2006 acquisition of

Scientific Atlanta. John T. Chambers has been CEO of Cisco since 1995 and Chairman of the Board since 2006. The Cisco logo has a series of blue vertical lines (going up and down, like a wave), which symbolise the info which Cisco sends over networks, while below this, the Cisco name is written in red capital letters.

The major Cisco slogan since October 2006 (Ogilvy and Mather, Culver City) is **"Welcome to the human network"** (with a variant **"Together we are the human network"**). A 1 minute 30 second TV ad from February 2009 illustrating this slogan shows shots of different places, all over the world. The shots are less important than the comments, "Welcome, welcome to a grand new day, to a new way of getting things done . . . Welcome to a place where maps are rewritten and remote villages are included . . . Where people subscribe to people, not magazines . . . Where books rewrite themselves . . . Welcome to the human network" (Executive Creative Director Karl Westman; Art Director Jeff Compton). In a shorter 32-second sequence (February 2007) one sees a father taking a photo of his son dancing – and sending this photo all over the world. One of the shots shows the North Seoul Tower[†] (777 feet above ground level). A third 1 minute 1 second ad (June 2009) shows a series of office people commenting to the tune of Glona Gaynor's "I Will Survive", "First I was afraid, I was petrified . . . Each meeting meant I would have to fly . . . but network video came along . . . Technology saved the day . . . More collaboration. Less complication. That's the human network effect".

CITROËN

Now part of the Peugeot–Citroën group, Citroën, initially founded in 1919 by André Citroën, is famous for the introduction of the DS19 (pronounced "Déesse", which is French for goddess) in 1955, and even more so for that of the 2CV ("Deux Chevaux", two horsepower) in 1948. The production of the 2CV lasted until 1990 but one can still see 2CV cars parked on the streets of Paris.

† *The author is grateful to Ms Victoria Davila Leis for this information.*

The most famous of Citroën's slogans is the French sentence **"Vous n'imaginez pas tout ce que Citroën peut faire pour vous"** – "You can't imagine what Citroën can do for you" (or the shorter **"C'est fou ce que Citroën. . ."** – "It's crazy what Citroën . . .). It was launched in 1993 at the same time as the Xanthia model, by Euro RSCG (RSCG, the initials of founders Bernard Roux, Alain Cayzac, Jacques Séguéla and Jean-Michel Goudard, who had been the advertising agent of Citroën since 1979).

Amongst the most recent slogans are **"Nothing moves you like a Citroën"** (2003, for the C3 model, conceived by Euro RSCG) and **"Créative Technologie"**, with both words written in French but in the Anglo-Saxon order.[†] This slogan was created by Agence H Paris (same group as Euro RSCG) in 2009 to celebrate the carmaker's ninetieth anniversary. The TV campaign accompanying the slogan focuses on the company's heritage and creativity. One of the very short 30-second films (February 2009) for this new slogan states: "Nowadays we're being told to reduce greenhouse gases, reduce CO2 emissions . . . reduce consumption . . . reduce danger, reduce stress, reduce noise . . . reduce costs . . . reduce, reduce, reduce . . . but there is one thing we'll never reduce: our creativity". The ad shows symbols of the various properties to be reduced, but ends with the Citroën logo and its two inverted Vs. The two chevrons of the logo symbolise the intermeshing contact of two helical gears in opposition – a logo which André Citroën used in the very early 1900s whilst also applying the concept industrially. Nowadays many people recognise the logo but very few know its origin.

CNN

Launched on 1 June 1980 from its headquarters in Atlanta, CNN (Cable News Network) has become in a short time one of the world leaders in 24-hour television news coverage. It is owned by Turner Broadcasting System, itself a subsidiary of Time Warner. CNN Worldwide's President is Jim Walton, who joined the network a year after it was founded, and its head of US operations is Ken

† Thank you to Marie Pitolin at Citroën France for part of this information.

Jautz. CNN's US network is in fierce competition with Fox News and MSNBC. The most famous programme on CNN may have been Larry King Live, where King interviewed celebrities from all avenues of life, which ended in December 2010. One of their renowned intrepid war reporters was Christiane Amanpour, who also left in 2010.

CNN has had a series of slogans which, except for the most recent one, place CNN in the race to be first to report. A very early 1991 slogan was **"Covering the world like nobody can"** (BBC World was launched that year but did not give full 24-hour coverage until later), followed by **"World's news leader"** (from 1992), and **"Be the first to know"** (March 2001 to September 2009). And indeed CNN were the first TV channel to announce the 9/11 attacks, showing one of the Twin Towers of the World Trade Center in flames. Their most recent slogan, **"Go beyond borders"**, was developed by CNN's global marketing and creative departments in collaboration with ad agency Tooth + Nail (Boston). It was launched on 21 September 2009 as the "Berlin Wall Tape Art Project" (Chief Creative Officer Guido Heffels and Creative Director Myles Lord), just before the twentieth anniversary of the Fall of the Berlin Wall. CNN marked 40km of red tape along the former East–West border, with the slogan repeated on each bit of tape. The taping was accompanied by eight art installations by Berlin artist El Bocho and the mapping done in collaboration with Google. Very recently CNN have been first again as reporter Nic Robertson found the location in Libya of Lockerbie bomber al-Megrahi.

COCA-COLA

The Coca-Cola company was founded in 1892 and is headquartered in Atlanta, Georgia; it has been chaired by Muhtar Kent (born in Turkey in 1952) since 1 July 2008. The star product, Coca-Cola drink, is somewhat of a legend and is a mix of caffeine (12.9mg per 100ml), sugar, phosphoric acid, carbonated water (which gives the drink its fizz), and highly secret natural flavourings, whose composition is apparently known to only two executives at a given time. The Coca-Cola drink itself was launched in 1886 by John Pemberton as a derivative of French "Wine Coca". Originally a mixture of cocaine and caffeine, Coca-Cola has been free of cocaine since 1904. The most well-known derivatives of Coca-Cola are caffeine-free "Free Coca-Cola", since 1983, and "Coca-Cola Zero", since 2005 – the latter has only 0.75 calories per bottle instead of the usual 140 calories, thanks to artificial sweeteners.

The Coca-Cola logo is the name of the beverage written with a special "Spencerian script", a rather sophisticated formal handwriting dating back to the mid-nineteenth century. There have been numerous Coca-Cola slogans over the years, from **"Refresh yourself"** (1924) and **"The pause that refreshes"** (1929), via **"Have a Coke"** (1979), and **"Always"** (1993–2000) to the contemporary **"Coke side of life"** (2006, Wieden & Kennedy, Amsterdam) and **"Open happiness"**, launched 9 January 2009 (McCann Erickson, Dublin), and even more recently **"Life begins here"** (2011). It is of course highly restrictive to choose a video for only one of all these slogans; yet I would like to mention the intriguing 2011 "Border" advertisement which lasts 1 minute 3 seconds. Two soldiers are standing on opposite sides of a somewhat mysterious desert boundary between two countries. One of the soldiers is relaxed and drinks Coca-Cola. The other soldier, however, is highly suspicious and it takes a lot of prodding from the first soldier to have him accept to share the drink. The lesson, of course, is that the love of Coca-Cola transcends boundaries. The very serious funereal music is by Handel ("Saraband in D minor", HWV 437).

DE BEERS

Founded by Cecil Rhodes in 1888 in Johannesburg, South Africa, and expanded with the help of the Rothschild family, presided by Ernest Oppenheimer from 1927 until his death in 1958, De Beers is now chaired by Ernest's grandson, Nicky Oppenheimer while its CEO since May 2011 is Philippe Mellier, former French President of Alsthom Transport. De Beers essentially has a corner on the market for rough diamonds, which are mined in South Africa but also in neighbouring Botswana and Namibia. Hence it is able to stabilise diamond prices by restricting supply. The reputation of the diamond business has long been tarnished by the production, in certain countries (Angola, Sierra Leone, etc) of "blood diamonds", ie diamonds mined in war zones and serving to finance insurgent or invading armies. The largest diamond ever found was the Cullinan diamond (3106.75 carats, ie 0.621 kilos), mined in 1905. Out of this stone nine major gemstones were cut, from Cullinan I (530 carats) to Cullinan IX (4.39 carats), all of which belong to the British Royal family, and also 96 smaller brilliants. The highest quality diamond is flawless D and the largest such cut diamond is the 273.85 carat Centenary diamond, apparently in private hands.

The famed slogan **"A diamond is forever"** was coined in April 1947 by Ms Frances Gerety, a copywriter for the US advertising firm N. W. Ayer & Sons. The story of her creation has been told repeatedly (see www.prnewswire.co.uk/cgi/news/release?id= 12285). This slogan is considered to be one of the best – if not *the* best – in advertising history. As to the price of diamonds, I was once told by a famous jeweller that "The price of diamonds never drops." I had bought a 1 carat flawless D diamond around 1977. A few years later the price of diamonds soared, only to collapse afterwards. I was fortunate to sell my diamond back . . . at my purchase price! At present the retail price of a cut internally flawless D-colour diamond is approximately £25,000 (see www.18carat.co.uk/onecaratdiamond.html).

DIESEL SPA

Whereas Nike and A & F pride themselves on being companies with a rich history, Diesel was more recently founded in 1978 by Renzo Rosso and Adriano Goldschmied in Molvena, near Vicenza (Italy). The young company had to play catch-up with its elder competitors; to do this Rosso had to distance himself from them. First of all he decided to sell jeans which were **"vintage"**, old-looking. The Diesel fabrication process thus goes as far as using special washes which fade out the colour (Golden Shade brand), rubbing a hole through the jean by hand and repairing it with patches (Golden Frost brand), or shooting random pellets of bleach at the jean (Golden Bullit brand), for the new **"Dirty New Age"** jeans.

Next, the advertising had to use provocative themes. The Diesel slogan, invented in 1991 by in-house international advertising director Maurizio Marchiori with Swedish group Paradiset (DDB's predecessor agency in Sweden), is **"For successful living"**. This slogan was relatively bland, and in recent years Diesel has attempted to draw attention through highly provocative ads. In 2009 the New York integrated ad agency Anomaly (Simons, Palmer, Clemmow and Carl Johnson) launched the **"Be stupid"** advertising campaign. The *a contrario* basic statement goes: **"Smart may have brains. But stupid has the balls. Be stupid – Diesel"**. The illustrations were very daring. The most striking still shows a young woman opening her bikini bottoms, looking down into them and taking a picture! A lion is growling in the background. The ads were banned in the UK by the Advertising Standards Authority, in spite of Anomaly protesting that the campaign was a "rallying call to do things differently from the accepted wisdom and to live a life less ordinary" (*Marketing Week*, 30 June 2010). Why not? I would tend to side with Anomaly. Yet Diesel left Anomaly after only nine months and in June 2010 chose Argentina's Santo as its new ad agency.

DUBAI

Dubai is one of seven Emirates which form the United Arab Emirates (UAE) federation (President, Khalifa bin Zayed Al Nahyan). It is situated on the Persian Gulf coast, with a population of approximately 2 million. Its monarch is Sheikh Mohammed bin Rashid Al Maktoum, and Islam is the official state religion. Dubai is essentially a tourist gateway for people travelling between Europe and Asia. The country boasts the world's highest building – the Burj Khalifa (Khalifa Tower), 828 metres or 2,717 feet high – although the top floor is only at 621 metres or 2,038 feet. The tower was designed by Chicago-based architects Skidmore, Owings and Merrill, and it was constructed by Samsung (see Samsung article on page 187). Its triangular base is inspired by the flower Hymenocallis or Desert Lily, yet not unique to that desert region. The name of the Khalifa Tower was chosen just before its inauguration on 4 January 2010, to honour and thank the UAE President whose financial support was crucial in having the construction completed.

In October 2010, the Dubai Tourism and Commerce Marketing Department (DTCM) launched a new and powerful slogan, **"Definitely Dubai"**, with a nice alliteration. The purpose is perfectly summarised by a 2 minute 38 second TV ad, broken up into four 30-second parts, each emphasising a Dubai tourist attraction: culture (in particular Dubai's own traditions); hospitality (the "warm welcome"); leisure ("Pamper yourself"); and – last but not least – shopping ("Shopper's Paradise", "World Brands"). The slogan appears at the end of each short sequence and is printed on two lines: above, the word **"definitely"** written in regular European lower case type; below, the word **"Dubai"** in Arabic "Tuluth" script – again symbolising the encounter of two civilisations. A long 13 minute 13 second TV ad accompanying the previous Dubai slogan – **"Freedom to do Business"** – emphasises the various "freedoms": "to grow", "to express", "to create", "to invest", and, last but not least, "freedom to do business".

FERRARI

Ferrari, founded by Enzo Ferrari in 1929, has been located in Maranello, 18km from Modena, since the early 1940s. The city houses the company headquarters, the Ferrari construction site and also the Ferrari Museum. Several Ferrari cars have been named after Maranello. Above all, Ferrari is famous for its racing cars (*Scuderia Ferrari* means "Ferrari Stable"), whose production started well before that of the street vehicles (Ferrari S.p.A.).

The Ferrari logo is a famous black prancing horse on a yellow background (yellow is the colour of Modena, where Enzo Ferrari was born), with three discrete horizontal lines, bearing the colours of Italy, at the very top.

Does Ferrari have a slogan? First of all, the term **"Approved"**, which appears in certain advertisements, is not really a slogan but the label for Ferrari used cars. But what about the famous slogan **"Beyond perfection"**? This slogan is definitely used by the "companion" company, ACER, the world's number three manufacturer of portable computers. Some ACER PCs have the Ferrari yellow horse logo on the PC cover. And ACER writes: "The all-new Ferrari One laptop, with its personalised racing red cover proudly displaying the *Scudetto Ferrari* that has dominated Formula One since the very first race . . .". Yet this slogan is definitely an ACER slogan, and was invented by senior copyrighter Michael Walsh for Circleline Communications in August 2009. As for Ferrari, they have no slogan, because the company is so proud it considers it doesn't need one. However, in its advertisements, the word **"Passion"** comes up a lot.

GUINNESS

Guinness is a stout, ie a dark beer, alcohol content 4%–7.5%, brewed with water, barley (a portion of which is roasted), hops (a vine plant used for flavouring), yeast which produces the fermentation, and traces of isinglass, a clarifying agent. The beverage was launched in 1759 by Arthur Guinness at the Saint James's Gate Brewery, Dublin – which is still the sole provider of Guinness. Like Baileys, Guinness belongs to Diageo PLC.

The Guinness logo is a "Brian Boru" harp, similar to that of the Irish coat of arms, but facing in the opposite direction. The most famous ad line is **"Guinness is good for you"**, which dates back to the 1920s. For a period there was a contention concerning this ad since, officially, alcohol could not be good for you. However, in the early 2000s it appeared that antioxidants in Guinness beer might reduce blood clots and slow down the deposits of cholesterol on the artery walls. Other slogans worth mentioning are **"My goodness, my Guinness"**, **"17.59. It's Guinness time"** (my favourite), and most recently the **"Good things come to those who. . ."** followed by an image of beer being poured into a Guinness glass. In the 1 minute 32 second video commercial (1999), a surfer on the beach starts slowly: "I don't care who you are – here's to your dream". He and his friends then surf in the midst of diving horses, water vortices and more and more intense drumming. They end back on the beach, "Here's to waiting!", and then the Guinness pint appears with the "Good things. . ." slogan. This commercial was created by Abbott Mead Vickers BBDO agency.

HEATHROW

Until now, communication does not seem to have been a major preoccupation of Heathrow Airport. Yet this airport is the busiest in Europe in terms of passenger traffic, and also handles more international passengers than any other airport in the world. It is owned and operated by BAA Limited (CEO Colin Matthews and Chairman Sir Nigel Rudd), itself a subsidiary of international consortium ADI Ltd. It has five terminals. Terminal 5 (exclusively used by British Airways) opened on 27 March 2008, barely four years ago. The airport handles 66 million passengers per year. The busiest international routes are New York JFK (2.52 million passengers), Dubai, surprisingly (1.78 million), Dublin (1.49 million) and Hong Kong (1.38 million). The oldest terminal, Terminal 2, is being refurbished and should reopen in 2014 for Star Alliance carriers (United Airlines, Lufthansa, etc) On 7 February 1996, a Concorde aircraft made a historic 2 hour 52 minute 59 second crossing from Heathrow to New York, the fastest ever transatlantic flight.

The history of Heathrow is full of amazing incidents. On 17 May 2004 Scotland Yard's Flying Squad foiled an attempt by seven men to steal £40 million in gold bullion plus an equivalent amount in cash from the Swissport Cargo Warehouse. More recently, on 18 December 2010 heavy snowfall caused the closure of the entire airport, and the situation took several days to resolve. . . In the most recent incident on 26 May 2011, a Middle East Airlines flight was held up for 7 hours (because it had lost its turn in the take-off rotation) without the passengers being able to disembark.

As for Heathrow's slogans, the most well-known until now may well be those used by protestors at the airport, "Climate camp – no airport expansion" (August 2007), or "Stop airport expansion" (March 2008). These campaigns seem to have been successful since on 12 May 2010, David Cameron's government abandoned the project of a sixth terminal and third runway. In June 2009 BAA Marketing, Insight Director Nick Adderley and his colleagues in Heathrow's Communication Team launched the slogan **"Making every journey better"**. Recently (October 2010) the T-Mobile phone company has run several TV ads at Heathrow Terminal 5 in which passengers are greeted very happily, with dancing and singing. A still at the beginning states "Heathrow T5. Welcome back", where the last two words could be a potent slogan.

HEINZ

The oldest and possibly most famous Heinz slogan is **"57 Varieties"**, though I have not seen it appear in TV ads in recent years. Apparently "5" and "7" were founder Henry John Heinz's lucky numbers. As of today, 57 remains the favourite number of Heinz, although the company has far more products worldwide. The CEO is William R. Johnson; the company is still headquartered in Pittsburgh where it was founded.

The most famous Heinz product in the western world is its tomato ketchup – now in a squeezable bottle with the subtitle "57 Varieties", and the picture of a tomato with the slogan **"Grown, not made"**. I would suspect that Heinz has a corner on the world market of tomato ketchup. They are definitely no. 1 in the USA, and they sell 650 million bottles a year, worldwide.

The slogan **"No one grows ketchup like Heinz"**, where again its word "grows" has the required implication, is due to McCann Erikson, London (December 2007). The more recent slogan **"It has to be Heinz"** (Abbott Mead Vickers BBDO, October 2009; Art Director Jim Seath), which focuses on Heinz Beanz, Heinz Tomato Ketchup, Heinz Salad Cream, plus pasta and soup, has apparently helped increase the sales of Heinz significantly. In a recent 39-second ad, people gather in various situations (barbecue,

Christmas table, a lady receiving a call from her mother while she stirs tomato soup), while the ad ends up with the **"It has to be Heinz"**.

HITACHI

Hitachi Ltd dates back to 1910, when Namihei Odaira began making small electric motors. In 1920 Odaira incorporated his company as Hitachi, Ltd. Currently the company is the largest of Japan's global electronic companies and has some 360,000 employees. The company has diversified into industrial machinery and power plants. The headquarters are in Chiyoda, Tokyo and the President (since 2010) is Hiroaki Nakanishi. Hitachi has no logo proper but has a **"Hitachi Tree"**, a Monkeypod tree curiously located in Monalua Gardens, Oahu, Hawaii, and which symbolises the "comprehensive drive", "wide business range" and "earth-friendliness" of the company.

Since April 2000 the Hitachi slogan is **"Inspire the next"** (the result of a worldwide competition for ideas launched by the Corporate Brand & Communications Division[1]). The "x" of the slogan branches slightly out to the right, symbolising Hitachi's resolve to take the lead in the times ahead, and has a small red acute accent symbolising the passion of all those who work under the Hitachi corporate brand. In a 39-second ad (March 2006) a young fellow proposes several dishes to his girlfriend. Each time she says "No!". An off-screen voice comments: "Choosy about your veggies? There's a special vegetable compartment that keeps lots of veggies farm-fresh for lots longer – only with the new Hitachi Kudo refrigerator". The fellow now pretends to refuse the fresh salad offered by the girl, but he quickly relents. The tagline is "Home and Life Solutions from Hitachi". In another superb 59-second ad in December 2006 **"Power Unleashed"** by Jean-Paul Goude, a leopard with a bejewelled leash is held by a beautiful lady in red dress. An off-screen voice: "The true power and beauty of plasma is often hidden, unable to be captured". The leopard keeps pulling

† Thank you to Mioka Suzuki, Hitachi Europe, for this information.

on the leash while snarling. Off-screen voice: "Only Hitachi
original technologies . . . unleash the most lifelike colour and detail
in plasma." The leopard finally breaks free as the jewels scatter, and
jumps right through the screen of a Hitachi TV! The tagline:
"Introducing the world's highest-resolution 42-inch plasma TV –
only from Hitachi". The beautiful music is by John Ottman and
was inspired by neo-tango band Gotan Project.

HONG KONG

Hong Kong is one of the dream places of the world, in spite of its
tiny size (1,100 square km). It has a population of 7 million; and
the Chief Executive since 2005 is Sir Donald Tsang. The transition
of Hong Kong from British rule (29 August 1842) to Chinese rule
(1 July 1997) was one of the most remarkable peaceful changes of
rule of the last century. Although a region of the People's Republic
of China, Hong Kong has a special statute with high autonomy
except foreign relations and military affairs. This is the so-called
"one country, two systems" principle. The Hong Kong flag itself has
a red background symbolising the mother country, but a central
white, five-petal *Bauhinia blakeana* local flower which symbolises
the city's specificity.

The excellent **"Live it. Love it"** Hong Kong slogan was discovered
by Clifford Ng in autumn 2003 while he was Creative Director at
Foote, Cone and Belding, and at a time when the city was making
an all-out effort to recover from the devastating SARS epidemic
(November 2002–July 2003). One of the TV ads (August 2006,
2 minutes 1 second) illustrating the slogan shows a series of Hong
Kong sites or events, with the series of catchwords: "Feel it!", "See
it!", "Wear it!", "Taste it!", "Win it!" (this word accompanies a horse
race finishing with an amusing incident where an occidental-
looking woman embraces a local-looking man as they celebrate
their victory), "Rock it!", "Swing it!". . . At the end, after promoting a
Buddhist shrine, an attraction park and sailors in the port, the ad
shows all the catchwords again (plus "Find it!") and, finally, the
slogan. Another later ad (May 2009, 2 minutes 1 second)

emphasises the **"Live it. Love it"** slogan even more, "Live the serenity", "Live the wonder", "Love the city", "Love the rush", "Love the tradition", "Love the Moments"... The slogan is recognised worldwide and remains a powerful tool of the Hong Kong Tourist Board.

IKEA

IKEA is a Scandinavian – Swedish to be more exact – success story. Someone who wishes to buy IKEA furniture first goes on the internet to browse the IKEA online catalogue, and next orders by email or visits one of the IKEA stores, generally far out on the outskirts of big cities, with their recognisable violet-blue colour and yellow store headlines. The IKEA company was founded in 1943 by Ingmar Kamprad at the age of 17 – hence the first two letters of the company name. Presently the Chairman and CEO is Thomas Bergström. The first IKEA store was launched in 1958 in Älmhult, Smaland, Sweden. The biggest stores (close to 50,000 square metres) are in Stockholm, Malmö, Shengyang (China) and Melbourne. IKEA is well-known for its eco-friendly behaviour. They developed an Environmental Action Plan in 1992 and launched the IKEA Green Tech capital venture fund in 2008. The 2012 catalogue will be presented in 59 editions in 31 languages and in 39 countries.

The most recent IKEA slogan, **"The life improvement store"**, was launched in 2010 by Ogilvy and Mather. In one 32-second TV ad (July 2011) the narrator says: "Rachel and Sam have a **house**; now they want a **home**. A home where everything feels like it's designed just for them. Where the styles they love fit into the budget they have... We're more than a home improvement store. We're IKEA, the life improvement store." The slogan has been accompanied by a "Life Improvement Project" with a $100,000 prize for the winner. The most recent winner was young Kyria Henry whose foundation "Paws4Vets" provides dogs for war veterans subject to post-traumatic stress.

INTEL

The Intel story can be qualified as a case where a company has become better known for its slogan than for its complex scientific products. The founding fathers on 18 July 1968 were scientists Gordon E. Moore and Robert Noyce together with venture capitalist Arthur Rock, and they were almost immediately joined by Andrew Grove, later to become CEO. The current President and CEO is Paul Otellini and the Chairman Jane Shaw. The company's logo, two semi-circles surrounding the name intel in lower case letters, is inspired by the original swirl logo developed by Steve Gregg with Grove.

If ever a slogan was near-perfect, the **"Intel inside"** (initially **"Intel. The computer inside"**) slogan (Dahlen, Smith, White, Salt Lake City, with Intel Marketing Manager Dennis Carter, 1991) is it. Indeed the two words follow each other with an excellent alliteration while the punch-word **"inside"** describes perfectly – if it were ever possible with a single word – what Intel essentially does, ie developing microprocessors, which are essential to computers. In 1998 Intel changed its ad agency to Messner Vetere Berger McNamee Schmetterer New York (a EURO RSCG subsidiary), and again in 2005 to McCann World Group. In March 2006 Intel vaunted its association with Apple in a 35-second ad. An off-screen voice comments, "The Intel chip: for years it's been trapped inside PCs, inside dull little boxes . . . when it could have been doing so much more. Starting today the Intel chip will be set free and get to live life inside a Mac. **Imagine the possibilities**" (for this tagline, see also the article on Samsung on page 188).

On 11 May 2009 Intel launched the **"Sponsors of Tomorrow"** slogan[†] with San Francisco ad agency Venables, Bell & Partners, founded and co-directed by Paul Venables. The fundamental idea was to promote Intel as a global brand and no longer as just a maker of microprocessors. Several TV ads accompanied the new slogan. One featured Ajay Bhatt, co-inventor of the USB key, with the tagline **"Our rockstars aren't like your rockstars"**. Another

---

† Thank you to David Dickstein, PR Manager at Intel, for much of the information.

lovely video, "Oops", shows dozens of Intel workers on their knees frenetically looking for a lost chip, just before a conference boasting "World Premiere . . . Intel's Smallest chip". One fellow, "OK. I've found it!". He holds the chip at the end of tweezers. Applause and photographs. And the tagline, **"Our big ideas aren't like your big ideas"**.

JAGUAR

Like many famous companies, Jaguar was originally created, not for making the cars which would give it fame, but for something only marginally connected to this. In 1922 the Swallow Sidecar Company was founded by Sir William Lyons to make motorcycle sidecars. On 9 April 1945 the name was changed to Jaguar Cars Limited – an excellent brand name which itself supersedes the slogans since the Jaguar is an animal which evokes speed and endurance. After belonging to Ford Motors from November 1989 to June 2008 Jaguar is now owned by Tata Motors, headquartered in Mumbai, India. The company headquarters are in Coventry. Jaguar owns the luxury Daimler brand as well as Rover and Lanchester.

Jaguar has had quite a few advertising agencies: Young & Rubicam succeeded J Walter Thompson in the autumn of 2001; Euro RSCG Worldwide succeeded Young & Rubicam in 2005 – they introduced the slogan **"Gorgeous"**, withdrawn however at the end of 2007; and most recently, since February 2011, there is Spark 44 (main principals Hans Riedel with Alastair Duncan, Steve Woolford, Bruce Dundore and Werner Krainz), located near Los Angeles and jointly owned by Jaguar itself. The most famous slogans are **"Don't dream it. Drive it"** (the oldest one), **"The art of performance"** (a J. Walter Thompson creation, used until early 2003) and **"Born to perform"** (introduced in 2004 by Young & Rubicam). In one former 1 minute 32 second TV ad (February 2008) for the **"Gorgeous"** slogan, a background voice repeats "Gorgeous, Gorgeous deserves your immediate attention, Gorgeous makes effort look effortless . . . Gorgeous can't be ordinary even if it tries . . . Gorgeous doesn't care at all what others

are doing . . . Gorgeous trumps everything, Gorgeous is worth it"
– accompanied by various short scenes: a couple hugging and a
woman pushing a man into a swimming pool!

KELLOGG COMPANY

Has any American child never tasted Kellogg's Corn Flakes? Or
Rice Krispies? Having been brought up in the USA, I became
accustomed to them during the World War Two years. At that time
(from exactly 31 August 1942 until 4 February 1949) Kellogg's were
already sponsoring "The Adventures of Superman" on the radio
and in comic books . . . Founded in 1898 by brothers John Harvey
Kellogg and Will Keith Kellogg as the Sanitas Food Company, then
in 1906 as the Battle Creek Toasted Corn Flake Company, the
Kellogg Company was finally renamed in 1922. Its present CEO
(since 2011) is John A. Bryant, while the Chairman of the Board is
James Jenness. The global headquarters are still in Battle Creek,
Michigan – also called the "Cereal City". Concerning Corn Flakes,
Kellogg's say they use "naturally sun-ripened corn that has been
growing in the fields for 120 days". But they also include quite a few
vitamins. As to Rice Krispies, famous for their **"snap! crackle! pop!"**
noise, their popularity makes Kellogg's the second largest importer
of rice in the UK. Other well-known company cereals are All-Bran
(not as popular with children because of their laxative purpose),
Coco Pops and Special K. Note that other famed cereals, such as
Cheerios, Quaker Oats, Shredded Wheat and Weetabix, are not
Kellogg's products.

The famous **"Sunshine Breakfast"** slogan dates back to at least
1958 and is due to the J. Walter Thompson ad agency. The Kellogg's
Corn Flakes jingle **"Good morning, good morning. The best to
you each morning. Sunshine Breakfast, Kellogg's Corn Flakes,
crisp and fun"** (the last verse has different versions – tune by Dave
Lee), inspired John Lennon and the Beatles' song "Good morning,
good morning" (Sgt Pepper album) in 1967. Recently (2009)
Kellogg's has turned to even shorter slogans, such as the
"wonderfully simple" ad for Rice Krispies (ad agency Leo
Burnett Ltd).

LEVI'S

The word Levi's is synonymous, in many people's minds, to blue jeans. Rightly so, since Levi Strauss – a Bavarian who had travelled to San Francisco in 1853 during the Gold Rush – and Jacob Davis obtained on 20 May 1873 the first US patent (US Patent 139,121) for blue jeans. At the beginning jeans were really overalls with braces. They were sold in San Francisco, which still hosts Levi's main store. The crucial characteristic was the material, called **denim**, from *serge de Nîmes*, a fabric made in that French city with its indigo-dyed blue colour. The first denim trousers date back to the sixteenth century in Chieri, Italy – they were exported through the port of Genoa, hence the name **"jeans"**.

The first Levi 501 R jeans were made in 1890, using denim from the Amoskeag Mill in Manchester, New Hampshire. Levi's has an interesting in-house booklet which shows how jeans evolved from 1890 till now, over a 120-year span. As vaunted in the London Regent Street roomy Levi's shop with its quiet atmosphere, "Each pair of 501 R jeans has 42 separate sewing operations to ensure it is crafted to perfection." Although Levi Strauss is not quoted on the stock market, *Time* magazine dubbed the 501 R jean the **"Fashion Item of the 20th Century"**.

The Levi's logo dates back to 1886, and shows two horses trying in vain to pull a pair of jeans apart. The 2008 jean, in a limited edition, still has the two-horse red leather patch on the back. The Levi's slogan, **"Go forth"**, is recent and was launched in the summer of 2009 by Wieden & Kennedy (Portland, Oregon), Levi's new ad agency. A 1 minute 2 second commercial (June 2009), filmed by Director Cary Fukunaga in black and white, is slightly over-patriotic since the comment (apparently a voice recording of Walt Whitman himself) glorifies America and tags onto Levi's **"Go forth"** banner and its red brand name only at the very end. Another July 2009 ad "Pioneers! O Pioneers!" is similarly over-patriotic.

LLOYDS TSB

The double name Lloyds TSB is a result of the relatively recent (1995) merger between Lloyds Bank, established in 1765 by John Taylor and Sampson Lloyd in Birmingham, and TSB Bank, dating back to only 1989 (see below). It is interesting that the Lloyds black horse logo dates back to 1677, when banker Humphrey Stockes set up his business in Lombard Street. It should be noted that the Lloyds prancing horse is not unlike the Ferrari one . . . Lloyds TSB was particularly hurt by the 2008–10 financial crisis, with an important UK government bailout. Lloyds has also been obliged by the European Commission to sell 632 branches (the "Verde" programme). On 30 June 2011, Lloyds Chairman Antonio Horta-Osorio announced that the company would shed 15,000 jobs in the 2011–14 period.

The TSB (short for "Trustees Savings Bank") part of Lloyds TSB is perhaps the more intriguing one. Savings banks, managed by voluntary trustees, had been used since 1810 (when the first such bank was created, and more formally since 1817 with the advent of the Savings Bank Act) to help poor people with low-volume and high-turnover deposits. In the second half of the twentieth century the decentralised structure of the TSB was abandoned, with final consolidation in the 1980s. TSB "bank" was created in 1989, but only to merge with Lloyds Bank a few years later, in a 30/70 per cent deal. TSB had had its own slogans since the 1970s – first **"TSB, it's the bank for me"**. Next, the 1979 slogan **"We like to say yes"** became in 1982 **"The bank that likes to say Yes"**.[†] In a recent TV film (December 2007), with actor David Boyce playing immensely rich JJ Hackenbush, the slogan is nicely shortened to **"TyesB"**.

The Lloyds **"for the journey"** slogan campaign, from the ad agency Rainey Kelly Campbell Roalfe/Y&R (Director Mark Craste, creatives Mark Waldron, David Godfree), was initiated in February 2007. One 1 minute TV ad (April 2007) shows a typical couple's "Life Journey"

---

† Thank you to Miss Anne Archer, from Lloyds Archives, for the information concerning these former slogans. However, nobody seems to know who invented the 1982 "the bank that likes to say yes" slogan.

– they meet on a train, later get married, and finally happily wave off their daughter and her fiancé: **"for the journey"** . . .

L'OREAL

Sometimes a company slogan is so powerful that, when seeing an ad vaunting that company, one immediately anticipates the slogan with which the ad will end – with even a slight fear that the company might, after all, have dropped the slogan! This is the case of L'Oréal, the world's largest cosmetics company, with its famed slogan **"Parce que je le vaux bien"** (in French), ie **"Because I'm worth it"**. Indeed a large number of people (apparently 71% of the female population in the USA) remember this slogan and can identify its origin. In recent years the company has introduced some variations, such as **"you're"**, **"we're"**, **"he's"** or **"she's"** instead of **"I'm"**.

L'Oréal's headquarters are located in Clichy, a suburb very close to Paris. My experience with L'Oréal – which once kindly offered me a job in their Research Centre in the eastern suburbs of Paris – is that they keep a low profile, nearly secretive attitude, possibly justified for a company with many research labs. Former CEO Sir Lindsay Owen-Jones, a British citizen with Welsh roots who chaired L'Oréal from 1988 until March 2011, can be credited with the fantastic worldwide development of L'Oréal. The company is owned 30.9% by Liliane Bettencourt, 29.7% by Nestlé and 36.8% by the general public.

The **"Because I'm worth it"** slogan was introduced as far back as 1973 and was originally intended for Préférence, a L'Oréal hair colour. As reported in *The New Yorker* article "True Colors" (22 March 1999, "Annals of Advertising" column), the slogan was discovered by Miss Ilon Specht, then aged 23, working as a copywriter at the McCann–Erickson advertising agency in New York. The commercial ran as follows, "I use the most expensive hair colour in the world, Préférence by L'Oréal. It's not that I care about money. It's that I care about my hair . . . What's worth more to me is the way my hair feels . . . I don't mind spending more for L'Oréal. **Because I'm worth it**". The slogan is now 38 years old.

M&M'S [MARS INCORPORATED]

M&M's are chocolates coated with a candy shell. They were created by Forrest Mars, Snr. and produced as of 1941 by him and Bruce Murrie. M&M's are amongst the most well-known Mars products; others include Uncle Ben's rice, Royal Canin and Whiskas . . . The current Mars CEO is Paul S. Michaels; the board of directors are all members of the Mars family. The slogan **"The chocolate melts in your mouth, not in your hand"** is a direct jibe at common chocolate bars (Hershey, Nestlé), which are prone to melt in your hand or even in your coat pocket. The M&M's slogan dates back to 1954 and originated from the Ted Bates Agency.

The six possible colours are **red, yellow, brown, green, orange** and **blue** – where the last two colours replace the original violet colour. I bought two packages of the three most common M&M's varieties in two different local Hammersmith stores:

- 45g yellow **"peanut"** packet (apparently the most popular in my two local shops): 2 vs 7 red, 3 vs 2 yellow, 4 vs 4 brown, 4 vs 4 green, 8 vs 1 orange, 0 vs 2 blue. The total is not constant from one packet to another – and one packet had no blue M & M's whatsoever!

- 36g blue **"crispy"** packet: 3 vs 8 red, 7 vs 10 yellow, 8 vs 8 brown, 8 vs 3 green, 4 vs 4 orange, 6 vs 2 blue. Totals: 36 and 35, but all six colours are present.

- 45g dark brown **"choco"** packet: 5 vs 7 red, 6 vs 10 yellow, 7 vs 9 brown, 12 vs 7 green, 7 vs 11 orange, 10 vs 5 blue. Totals: 47 and 49 – but again all six colours are there.

Hence one cannot be guaranteed that all six colours are present in a given small packet; also, although the weights are certainly correct, the actual number of sweets varies from one packet to another!

MERCEDES-BENZ

Mercedes-Benz, a division of Daimler AG, is the oldest car manufacturer still in existence; its origin dates back to 1886, with the creation by Karl Benz of the first petrol-powered car. The Mercedes-Benz headquarters are in Stuttgart and the company also produces trucks and buses. The head of the Mercedes-Benz Cars Division is Dieter Zetsche, who is also CEO of Daimler; while Manfred Bischoff is Chairman of Daimler's Board. Mercedes-Benz, which had for a long time specialised in the top and more expensive range of the car market, has also been successful with its mini Smart two-seater model. Mercedes was not a Greek or Roman goddess, but the female hero of Alexandre Dumas' novel *The Count of Monte-Cristo*, whose English translation was first published in 1846. So the car brand was really named after a woman! (According to www.cybersteering.com, the head of Daimler Cars for Austria, Hungary, France and the USA had a daughter called Mercedes – probably inspired by the popular novel – and the name was registered in 1902).

First launched in 1997, Mercedes used the slogan **"Falling in love again"** (Lowe & Partners/SMS, New Jersey). The famed **"Unlike any other"** slogan was introduced in March 2002 by Merkley, Newman, Harty & Partners, New York. There are many videos illustrating this slogan, which was still active in 2010. One is a 32-second spot, "Crash Test" (November 2007), which shows a G-Class SUV taking off in the test room with dummy models at the wheel. As it hits the wall, it crashes through it and also through the next room until it arrives outdoors. One hears a shout, "Hey! What are you guys doing there?!". At the end, of course, there is the Mercedes slogan.

The latest slogans for the company are **"The best or nothing"**, introduced in June 2010 (Shalmor Avnon Amichay/Y&R Interactive, Tel Aviv) and **"Welcome"** in February 2011 (Merkley & Partners, New York).

NESPRESSO

The recent fame of Nespresso (a unit of Nestlé Group, Switzerland) has arisen in two steps. First, around 2000, Nestlé introduced a new coffee machine which simply requires the heating of water and the insertion of aluminium capsules – which create a significant waste problem – carrying a specific coffee brand. The coffee then pours straight out of the machine. There are 16 such brands, which Nestlé calls "Grands Crus", in a rather far-fetched reference to wines. These 16 brands are three "Decaf" brands, three "Lungos", three "Pure Origin" (one each from India, Brazil and Colombia) and seven different "Espressos".

The second defining moment was the appearance of George Clooney (October 2006) in a series of now-famous Nespresso ads. In the very first one (51 seconds; McCann Paris, directed by Bennett Miller) Clooney enters a Nespresso shop to have a cup of coffee. Two young women sitting at a nearby table make comments seemingly directed at him: "Dark!", "Very intense . . .", "Unique", "Mysterious. . .", "Strong character . . .", "Very rich!", "Deep and sensual . . .". Clooney gets closer to them, "You're talking about Nespresso, right? Yeah What else? **Nespresso, what else?**", "OK", say the disappointed women.

But the most famous clip is the November 2009 ad (McCann Erickson Paris; filming by Robert Rodriguez via Moonwalk Films) in which Clooney leaves a Nespresso shop with a newly-bought Nespresso machine – but a piano falls on him from the upper floors. Thus we see Clooney climbing clouded steps to heaven, where he meets God (John Malkovich):

"Hello, George! "

"Where am I?"

"Make an educated guess" says God (a lovely phrase!)

"It must be a mistake!"

"We don't make mistakes, ever!"

"See, it's not my time" Clooney protests.

"Maybe we could make an arrangement?!"

Clooney looks down at his parcel and says: "It has to be the coffee maker?". After attempting to lure God into accepting other offers (a Porsche, a house on Lake Como), Clooney gives up and hands the coffee machine over to God. He finds himself again in front of the shop, but the piano falls behind him!! The Nespresso slogan ends the clip.

NIKE

Nike Inc. is named after the Greek goddess of victory (for a famous statue of this goddess, see the "Winged Victory of Samothrace" at the Louvre Museum, Paris). The company was founded on 25 January 1964 by Phil Knight (still Chairman of the Board today) and by his athletics coach at the University of Oregon, Bill Bowerman, as Blue Ribbon Sports. The company name was switched to Nike in 1978, but it had already been selling Nike football shoes since the summer of 1971. The current CEO is Mark Parker, and the company headquarters are in Beaverton, Oregon. Nike has owned Converse since 2003. The famous Nike logo is called a "swoosh", a sort of checkmark, and can be red, white or black. It was created in 1971 by Carolyn Davidson, a graphic design student at Portland State University, who later was graciously thanked by Knight. This goes to show, if it were necessary, that a single streak of imagination can lead to great fame.

Many famous athletes, not least of which Michael Jordan, have helped to promote Nike. But it's the slogan **"Just do it"** which has been most helpful. It was created in 1988 by Dan Wieden (of Wieden & Kennedy, Nike's ad agency since 1982) during a brainstorming session (see also www.cfar.com/Documents/nikecmp.pdf). In a somewhat mysterious 30-second TV ad (April 2005: Wieden & Kennedy, Portland, Oregon; Creative Directors Hal Curtis and Mike Byrne) one sees athletes running barefoot on a sandy beach. They are all in white. Suddenly the beach becomes littered with city objects: mailboxes, fire hydrants, until the onlooker finds himself looking in a city at a grey-shirted runner with a red pair of Nike's. The tagline is **"Run Barefoot"** and is intended to promote the "Nike Free" shoe series. Nike, contrary to

Adidas, was not an official sponsor of the last two football World Cups but it sponsors some of the leading national teams. In May 2010 it launched a 3-minute ad, with tagline **"Write the Future"**, in which it celebrates epic football moments and players.

NOKIA

Nokia has been a flagship for Finland. Founded in 1865 by Frederik Idestam as a pulp mill company – with one mill located near the town of Nokia in south-east Finland – the Nokia company was launched in 1871 by Idestam and partner Leo Mechelin. Presently the headquarters are in Espoo, near Helsinki. Nokia went into the mobile phone business first in 1966, with car phones, next with the "Mobira Talkman", a transportable phone, and finally with the first GSM phones in 1992 (Nokia 1011). With GSM, not only could one talk, but also one could send text messages (SMS – short message service), listen to music or send pictures. In spite of its leading position in the field of mobile phones during the 2000–10 period, Nokia is said to have missed the "smartphone" revolution, which required sophisticated software, rather than hardware, to use the phone also as a computer (Wi-Fi connectivity, for instance). The company has thus suffered a declining market share.

Nokia has no logo properly speaking, other than the name Nokia accompanied by the company slogan. The latter, **"Connecting people"**, was introduced in 1992 by Ove Strandberg. At the time the slogan was introduced, writes Strandberg, "I was doing my thesis . . . at Helsinki University of Technology . . . and working part time at Nokia Research Centre . . . I remember that I was so tightly wound up writing the thesis that I reflected that a break of half an hour would do me good. Thus I played along with some slogan versions that ended up with **"Nokia connecting people"** and **"Connecting Nokia people"**." Strandberg then submitted his two slogans to the Research Centre. Nokia HQ later shortlisted the first one and finally selected it in November 1992. This story goes to show, if it were ever needed, that finding a good slogan doesn't necessarily require an ad agency. However, the capacity to put an idea through to the general public, ie popularisation, is a privilege for the happy few.

The slogan is written in a special font designed in 2002 by German designer Erik Spiekermann. The ringing tune for Nokia phones is easily recognisable. Quite a few Nokia video ads are "still" ads, concentrating almost exclusively on the phone. However, even a company as low profile as Nokia couldn't resist the trend towards more sexy commercials. Thus a recent video ad made by David Wilson for the Nokia N8 Pink, with music by the Sugababes ("Freedom"), stars a giant pink deer and several dancing dolls, which move around like puppets in a puppet show. At the very end, the main puppet wears a bra made of two Nokia phones.

PATEK PHILIPPE

Patek Philippe was founded in 1851 by Pole Antoine Norbert de Patek, who had been making pocket watches for more than a decade, and French watchmaker Adrien Philippe, inventor of a keyless winding system which allowed you to pull out a button to set the clock and push it back in to wind the clock. They had met in 1844 at the Paris Universal Exhibition. The current President of the Board is Thierry Stern, who succeeded his father Philippe in August 2009. The CEO is Claude Peny. The company headquarters are in Geneva, and the factory in Plan-les-Ouates, some 3 miles away. The company is privately held by the Stern family. The two most expensive watches ever sold at auction were both Patek Philippes: a "Supercomplication" 1932 pocketwatch ($11 million at Sotheby's New York in December 1999) and a 1943 "Perpetual Chronograph" sold at Christie's Geneva in May 2010 for 6.26 million CHF (the dollar was then worth 1.1 CHF).

The Patek Philippe slogan **"Begin your own tradition"** dates back to 1996 and was coined by Tim Delaney at ad agency Leagas Delaney.[†] Its emphasis is on "legacy" and on "intemporality". An

---

† *Thank you to Margaret Johnson, Group CEO at Leagas Delaney London, for this info.*

interesting 10 minute 6 second ad (January 2008, directed by Remi Faillant; producer Emmanuel Ryz; photography Claude Esselen; music Eric Mouquet) tells a story of such family legacy involving a Patek Philippe "Calatrava" watch engraved *"A mon fils"* (in French: to my son) on the back. The watch is being sold at the Drouot – Montaigne auction house in Paris. As the auction proceeds, the history of the watch is being told by the successful-bidder-to-be. When he was 20 years old, his father gave him the watch; later he apparently sold it, "Today I'm over 50 and I would like to rectify an error of my youth". The successful bidder – none other than the former youngster – will now give the watch to his son. Then the conclusion: "So the story of Patek Philippe goes on . . . Everyday in Geneva another chapter unfolds. . .". At first I found this story to be somewhat far-fetched until I remembered having myself sold to a close family friend the Patek Philippe wristwatch which my father had bequeathed to me – and also knowing that my recently deceased brother has bequeathed to my eldest son the Patek Philippe watch which I gave him for his birthday nearly 50 years ago! (You should bear in mind, however, that, in the field of watches as in any other field, the notion of "greatest" watches is not immutable, see www.verybestwatch.com.)

PETER JONES & JOHN LEWIS PARTNERSHIP

The Peter Jones store in Sloane Square, London, was bought in 1905 by John Lewis, founder of a department store in Oxford Street; it is a flagship of the John Lewis store chain. The John Lewis holdings have expanded since then and there are now some 30 department stores in the UK. They are the third largest private UK company. The Managing Director of Peter Jones is Tony Wheeler and the Chairman is Charlie Mayfield. I had the pleasure of discussing the unique nature of John Lewis stores with Rachael James, Marketing Manager at Peter Jones in the Department of Visual Merchandising. Ms James is in charge of a relatively new feature, **"Retailtainment"**, whereby she holds events in the store to advertise products to customers.

Two important features distinguish John Lewis stores. First, they try hard to strictly apply their 1925 slogan **"Never knowingly undersold"** (called "NKU" in-house!), nowadays accompanied by the tagline **"on quality, price and service"**. This somewhat cumbersome main slogan was introduced by John Spedan Lewis, son of the chain's founder. Indeed Peter Jones has an excellent policy of reimbursing or satisfying customers who have suffered a mishap. "We bend over to satisfy customers", says Ms James. In my personal case Peter Jones replaced the entire base of a double bed I had purchased because one of its drawers was not functioning properly. Second, all employees are **"partners"**, and the company is fully owned by its employees. There are no John Lewis shares proper, but each year part of Peter Jones' profits (in recent years 12%–15%), as with all John Lewis Partnerships, goes to employees. The other part serves for refurbishing, marketing, etc. Note that the percentage calculation is made on the entire John Lewis company so that every partner, whatever the efficiency of the store they work in, gets the same percentage.

An April 2010 John Lewis 1 minute 31 second TV ad shows the life of a woman, from birth to marriage to old age. It deals, albeit lightly, with how furniture comes into her life – from the crib at birth to the wedding sofa . . . In addition to the usual slogan, the film ends with **"Our lifelong commitment to you"**. The music is Billy Joel's "She's always a woman". The ad agency is Adam & Eve, London (Co-founder James Murphy, Creative Director Ben Priest, Art Director Ben Tollett).

According to Archivist Judy Faraday, to whom I am grateful for this information, the slogan took several forms, this one being the most concise and long-lasting

PROCTER & GAMBLE (P&G)

Founded in Cincinnati, Ohio (where it is still located) in 1837 by Englishman William Procter and Irishman James Gamble (who had married two sisters) with the purpose of selling candles and soap, P&G has now become a multi-billion-dollar giant. Some 23 brands each have billion-dollar sales. Out of the 23, the 10 which

I've personally used or heard of most (but another author might make a different choice) are Gillette (manual razors), Braun (electric shavers), Ariel (laundry detergent), Head & Shoulders (shampoo), Pampers (disposable baby diapers/nappies which date back to 1956), Duracell (batteries), Olay (women's skin care), Clairol (women's hair colour), and Always and Tampax (women's sanitary products). The current Chairman of P&G is Bob McDonald. There are now more than 120,000 employees worldwide. Five of the 11 board members are women.

P&G is a "company of brands" claiming to be dedicated to its customers. The slogan **"Touching lives, improving life"** has long been P&G's. It was launched in 2002 by Saatchi & Saatchi where it was created by Richard Holt. A 43-second ad (2009) starts by stating "For us it's always been about people, and taking care of what matters to them . . .". One sees successively a father shaving and joking with his very young son whose face is full of shaving cream, a cat eating IAMS pet food (another P&G product – although certain IAMS dog foods had to be recalled in 2011) while a dog jealously looks on, two girls brushing their teeth, children washing their hands . . . The conclusion, **"Even the simplest idea can build a better world"**. In March 2011 Wieden & Kennedy, Portland, Oregon launched the tagline **"Proud sponsors of mums"** (Creative Directors Danielle Flagg and Karl Lieberman). A 30-second film shows a sequence of still shots of children with their mother, but whose face is always hidden from the camera ("Mom is out of the picture").[†] The comments are shown on other stills: "She's the hands. She's the feet. She's the body without a head. Never the focus but always there. Like air. You couldn't breathe without her. Thank you Mum".

ROLEX

The Rolex company was founded on 15 November 1915 by two brother-in-laws, Hans Wilsdorf (born in Berlin) and Alfred Davis, who had already been working together on making wristwatches. Tradition has it that the "ex" of Rolex comes from the French word

† Thank you to Katie Abrahamson (W&K) for this info.

"exquise" (exquisite). Like Patek Philippe (see article on page 183) the company is owned privately; its new Chairman since May 2011 is Italian-born Gian Riccardo Marini. Amongst the famed Rolex watches are the first airtight, dustproof and waterproof "Oyster" watch (1926), the first self-winding "Perpetual" watch (1931), the first date-display "Datejust" watch (1945), and the first wristwatch to show simultaneously two time zones – the "GMT Master", created at the request of Pan Am Airways (1954; the GMT Master has a revolving rim, calibrated into 24 hours, with a special needle pointing to it). During World War Two, Wilsdorf offered Rolex watches to captured British officers in German camps, which were to be paid for only after the war. The gold crown Rolex logo was registered as early as 1925, but not used till 1939. The Rolex name is written in green capital letters or in white on a green background.

Although Rolex has sported quite a few slogans (see slogan list on page 97 and also the HEC Lausanne Thesis by Karine Gautschi, *www.hec.unil.ch/cms_irm/Gautschi.pdf*, section 8.2), most Rolex TV ads end up without a slogan showing up. An exception is **"A crown for every achievement"** (J. Walter Thompson, New York 2002), which ends several short ads featuring Roger Federer (a 13-second one in May 2007 and a 31-second mid-June 2010 one for the Wimbledon championship, where . . . Federer was eliminated on 30 June in a quarter-final). In 2011 a new slogan, **"Live for greatness"**, was introduced by Rolex (again J. Walter Thompson, New York). A new 30-second TV June 2011 ad with Federer, asks: "When is greatness achieved? . . . Maybe it's when you're always asking yourself 'What's next?'" The ad ends with the slogan.

SAMSUNG

Samsung is one of the world's largest electronics firms and is the second largest producer of mobile phones. It was founded in 1938 by Lee Byung-chull as a grocery and noodle producer. Its headquarters are near Seoul, South Korea. The current Chairman and CEO, after a 2-year interim, is Lee Kun-hee. Samsung is also a major shipbuilder and has an important construction branch (see article on Dubai on page 164). I personally own a Samsung SQ01 flat-panel TV. The Samsung logo has evolved from the original three-star logo (in Korean, the word Samsung means tristar) to the current bold-faced horizontal Samsung in a slanted light-blue oval-shaped background.

Over the last decade Samsung has been one of the most generous companies in terms of creating slogans for its products. As from 2002 the main slogan was **"everyone's invited"** and TV ads emphasised Samsung's digital technology. Since 2010 the slogans have multiplied, each one excellent in its own way. The slogan **"Turn on tomorrow"** concludes a nice 1 minute 2 second TV ad with Australian-born actor Simon Baker (music by Morgan Van Dam company, London). Actually one statement in the film, **"Tomorrow is delivered today"**, would have been an excellent slogan on its own. Another 2 minute 2 second TV ad advertising the Samsung Galaxy Tablet 10.1 glorifies various sports (starting with American football) and ends by stating: "Everything is possible for your imagination. **Imagine the possibilities**". A very recent slogan for the Samsung Notebook is **"Designed to go. Powered to perform"**. Last but not least, a superb 1 minute 44 second (9 September 2010) film by The Viral Factory (Shoreditch, UK), directed by Jake Lunt and promoting the Galaxy 580, shows a little girl dancing happily on her own in a gym. Two adults nearby are so impressed that they join in – and then two more. Finally the back of the room opens up to show the entire town dancing along with the little girl. The slogan is **"Use your influence"** with the Galaxy promo below it.

This phrase was also used as tagline in TV commercials introducing the use of the Intel chip in the new Mac computer line.

SAVE THE CHILDREN

Save The Children (STC) is a worldwide non-governmental organisation which helps support children, mainly in developing countries or in countries stricken by war or a meteorological disaster. However, it also helps poor children in the UK. STC was founded on 15 April 1919 by two British women, Eglantyne Jebb and Dorothy Buxton, with the purpose of helping children in post-war Germany and Austria-Hungary. STC was instrumental in obtaining the adoption by the UN General Assembly of the 54-article **"Convention on the Rights of the Child"**. The CEO of the International STC Alliance (29 countries) is Janine Whitbread. The CEO of STC UK is Justin Forsyth, and the Chairman of the UK Board of Trustees is Alan Parker. Finally the USA CEO is Carolyn Miles, who replaced Charles F. MacCormack in June 2011.

The Adam & Eve London ad agency was appointed to handle the STC account in April 2010, while John Ayling & Associates were awarded the media planning. In January 2011 a potent slogan, **"No child born to die"** (a group creation) was launched together with an ad campaign. A 1-minute TV ad directed by Chris Palmer (Gorgeous Production Co), and filmed in a Tanzanian village, features celebrities (Einstein, Mandela, several sportsmen) with a supporting commentary by actress Helena Bonham Carter. **"We are all born to be the fastest, the greatest or simply the 'bestest'[sic]. But while some are born to grow old and wise, many more will never grow up at all"**. The ad starts by showing a mother and child near a rail track in a shanty town and finishes with a child abandoned on the doorsteps of a house. Then a slide says: "Over 8 million children under 5 die needlessly every year" . . . Another 3 minute 28 second ad starts off with "WHAT . . . WERE YOU . . . BORN TO DO? . . . " and later states "No child should be born without a chance . . . Every child has the potential to shine . . . They just need a chance". As worldwide CEO Janine Whitbread states in a 27 January 2011 interview with Executive Editor Edie Lush of Hub Culture in Davos, "This is a marathon, not a sprint".

SONY

Sony, although a Japanese name, is one of the best-known brands in the Western world. It was founded by Akio Morita and Masaru

Ibuka in 1946 as a transistor company, and the name Sony was chosen in 1958. Since that pioneering period the company has turned into the world's fifth largest media conglomerate, under the name Sony Group. Amongst the most well-known business operations are Electronics (in particular TV sets), Games (PlayStation video games) and Sony Pictures Entertainment (movies – the latter created by acquisition of Columbia Pictures in 1989, and the legendary Metro-Goldwyn-Mayer Hollywood studio in 2005). The PlayStation is now in its third generation – judging by my own children and grandchildren, it is most popular with children aged 8 to 12, the teens switching over to Microsoft's Xbox. Last but not least, Sony's TV sets have a reputation of outstanding quality, even though they are slightly more expensive than their European counterparts. Sony's current Chairman is Sir Howard Stringer, a dual UK-US citizen.

In the past 10 years, Sony has come up with three successive and potent slogans. First, in April 2000, Saatchi & Saatchi launched **"Go create"**. In a 2007 TV commercial for the Sony VAIO laptop notebook, a lady undresses and literally jumps on a man who protests loudly – no wonder since they are being audited by the company's executives! In 2005 the slogan **"like.no.other"** was the subject of several outstanding TV ads for the Sony Bravia television brand, both by Fallon Agency in London. In the award-winning 2 minutes 27 seconds ad, millions of coloured balls fall along a San Francisco street, ending up as a "fog" of balls. At the very end, the word "colour" comes up, followed by **"like.no.other"** and **"BRAVIA, new LCD Television"**. A shorter 1 minute 11 seconds ad has geysers of coloured paint exploding around San Francisco buildings. It ends with cleansing rain and the same words. Finally, in September 2009, Agency 180 Los Angeles launched the actual slogan **"make.believe"**. "Believe that anything you can imagine you can make real", says the company in a 1 minute 32 second ad (November 2009). However, the troublesome aspect of this slogan is that "make-believe" – admittedly with a hyphen rather than a dot, and admittedly a noun rather than a verb – implies pretence, a false appearance ("pretending that what is not real is real", Merriam-Webster). So somehow I am not sure this ad will survive very long.

SUNDAY TIMES

The Sunday Times is a weekly newspaper founded in 1821 as *The New Observer* – its name changed a year later to the present one. In 1981 it was bought by News International and now belongs to Rupert Murdoch's news empire. John Witherow has been Managing Editor since 1995. The paper has a vast coverage of topics, including news (and comment), sport, business, news review, culture, style, travel and a magazine. Since June 2010 *The Sunday Times* charges for access to its pages via the internet. It would be interesting to know, after more than a year, how this decision has affected readership of both the paper version and the internet version. It has appeared recently that *The Sunday Times* may have been involved in the hacking of former UK Prime Minister Gordon Brown's family's private information.

After slogans such as **"Sunday isn't Sunday without The Sunday Times"** and **"The Sunday Times *is* the Sunday papers"**, advertising agency CHI & Partners, created by Simon Clemmow, Johnny Hornby and Charles Inge, launched in July 2008 the slogan **"For all you are"**. Associated with the launch was a remarkable 1 minute 1 second TV ad played by actor Peter O'Toole. As he walks with *The Times* newspaper tucked under his arm, he says, "In my life . . . I've been the hero . . . Once or twice I've been the villain . . . Sometimes I've enjoyed being the fool . . . In my life I have been many men and every now and then I've done a bit of acting [he chuckles]". Then another voice states **"The Sunday Times. For all you are"**. The piano music is by Pete Droge. CHI agency can also be credited for the recent daily *Times* slogan: **"Be part of the time"**.

SWATCH

The present Swatch Group originated in 1983 from the fusion of two ailing Swiss watch companies, German-speaking ASUAG (Allgemeine Schweizerische Uhrenindustrie AG) and French-speaking Swiss SSIH (Société Suisse pour l'Industrie Horlogère), under the guidance of Lebanese-born Nicolas George Hayek. Hayek launched the strategic concept of a plastic wristwatch with quartz movement aimed at the lower tiers of the watch market, and the first such Swatch (short for "second watch") watches were produced on 1 March 1983. Hayek became majority holder of the company in 1985 and renamed it SMH (Société Suisse de Microélectronique et d'Horlogerie) in 1986. The Swatch company name came later, in 1998. Hayek, called the "saviour of the Swiss watch industry", is credited with transforming the company into currently making 25% of total world watch production and 10% of sales. Hayek later diversified into cars and co-produced the "Smart" car with Mercedes. The Swatch Group owns famous brands such as Bréguet, Blancpain, Omega, Longines, Tissot . . . The current CEO, since 2003, is Nick Hayek, son of the founder.

The Swatch slogan is **"Shake the world"**, with an emphasis on spontaneity. It was introduced in autumn 2005 by Joshua G2 Agency, London, where it was created by Matthew House. In one of the first TV ads (1 minute 10 seconds, March 2007, with the background song "Cash the Thrill" by Kathy Dennis and Ben Cullem) you can see people standing to attention in a European city – whether they be on benches, desks, car roofs or in trees. An off-screen voice: "Hold your breath" . . . "This could be the perfect time" . . . "Is it now?". Suddenly, as a watch needle reaches the appropriate time, the Swatch slogan appears briefly and everybody jumps at the same time. Then Asian views – cyclists swerving and blossoms blowing away from a willow tree – show up. They are meant to demonstrate the impact of all those simultaneous jumps on the other side of the Globe. In another 31-second TV ad (June 2007), "Breathe" by Italian Director Francesco Nencini, a man tries to undo the blouse of a woman as they sit together on a couch. After 30 seconds he hasn't managed to do it and she throws him off! The Swatch comment: "Time is what you make of it."

The name of the person who coined the term "Swatch" remains a mystery.

TAMPAX

Tampax was for a long time an independent company located in Palmer, Massachusetts, and was bought only in 1997 by Procter & Gamble (see the P&G article on page 185). Tampax is the leader of the tampon market in the USA.

In 2008, thanks to Leo Burnett ad agency (Chicago & Milano), P&G launched a new slogan for Tampax **"Outsmart Mother Nature"**. One lovely 29-second spot (Leo Burnett with Digitas, London; media agency SMG United, extended to 46 seconds in 2009) starts by showing a beautiful young lady in white, shooting an ad with a handsome male partner. Suddenly Mother Nature appears – she wears a very strict green Chanel dress – with a small red box, "Having fun, anyone?" The young lady answers, "Mother Nature, *not now!*". "I brought you your monthly gift, Sweetie. You know, *your period!* I think you better stop shooting right now." The young lady answers, "Actually we can stay – I've heard of Pearl". Mother Nature, "Pearls, I invented them Darling!". "Not this one" . . . And then an off-screen voice, "Tampax invented Pearl, with the extraordinary Pearl Protect System . . .", followed by the slogan. In this and related ads Mother Nature is a "villain of sorts". The ad pitches her against independent "blue-blooded girls", as Sinatra would say. A Leo Burnett executive says, "The challenge really resonates with younger girls, because when someone tries to tell them how to lead their life . . . they want to outsmart that person" (see www.salon.com/life/broadsheet/2009/03/24/tampax).

Another 1 minute 1 second ad pits Mother Nature against . . . Serena Williams. It ends with Mother Nature, with her monthly gift, being volleyed off the tennis court by Williams!

TESCO

Tesco, one of the largest retailers in the world and the grocery market leader in the UK, is located in Cheshunt, Broxbourne, Hertfordshire. Its current Chairman is David Reid and its CEO since 2010 is Philip Clarke, who was the successor of Sir Terry Leahy. The company was founded in 1919 by Jack Cohen, who created the name Tesco by adding the first two letters of his surname to the initials of T.E. Stockwell from whom he had purchased a shipment of tea. The company has more than 5,000 stores worldwide.

Since autumn 1992/spring 1993, the Tesco slogan has been **"Every little helps"**, which followed **"Quest for Quality"**. This new slogan, due to the Lowe Lintas ad agency (Frank Lowe, Director), has been very successful in spite of its somewhat faulty grammar. Indeed "little" is an adjective and not a noun so the slogan is lacking a noun as subject for the verb "helps". This slogan, in my view, can be interpreted in two ways: 1) every customer purchase brings that customer a saving, however small; 2) it implies better service from the Tesco employees – who actually were given a DVD to adapt to the slogan. As Simon Edwards, then Marketing Director of Cobra Beer Products pointed out in 2006, the slogan implies "that no matter how big the company is they need to think at the same level as every single person walking through the door".

The new slogan was made popular by TV ads starring Prunella Scales (as Dotty, over-zealous) and Jane Horrocks (as her daughter Kate). In one 42-second ad (9 January 2009), Dotty buys all the toilet paper in a Tesco store – "let's stock up while the price is this low". To which a Tesco commentator answers, "At Tesco we try to make sure our low prices stay low, which means you can relax!". The slogan ends the film.

TIFFANY & CO.

Although Tiffany's may not have been involved with providing diamonds to royalty (like De Beers see page 162), it has its own historical fame. Founded in 1837 by Charles Lewis Tiffany and Teddy Young, the store was initially dedicated to stationery. In 1853 it took its present name and emphasis on jewellery. In 1879 Charles Lewis Tiffany bought a giant 287.42 yellow diamond from De Beers and had it cut into a cushion-shaped 128.51 carat diamond which is still a standard-bearer for Tiffany's. It is generally on display on the ground floor of their flagship store on 57th Street & 5th Avenue in New York. The current Chairman since 2002 and CEO since

1998 is Michael J. Kowalski. There are now Tiffany stores worldwide. In London alone there are three central stores, plus the Westfield store, and one at Heathrow Terminal. Tiffany's avoids at all costs being looked upon as catering only to older or richer women. The Westfield store is often packed with young clients.

In recent years Tiffany's have added to their **"New York since 1837"** slogan, which claims, like certain watchmakers do, that company age is a criterion of quality. The slogan **"Some style is legendary"** (which, in a sense, also refers to longevity) appeared in 2008. In a series of stills, some seven top models each wear a different set of jewels; each still is accompanied by the slogan. Note that in this, like in other ads, Tiffany's touches lightly on the jewels – no zoom or anything – whether they be engagement rings, necklaces or bracelets. None of the TV ads I've seen have any talking – only background music. A March 2008 ad, showing off rings on playful blonde Julia Stegner and quiet dark-haired Ethiopian Liya Kebede, ends with **"There are times to celebrate"**. In December 2009 a new slogan, **"Give voice to your heart"**, appeared. Last but not least one must mention the *Breakfast at Tiffany's* 1961 movie, directed by Blake Edwards and based on a novel by Truman Capote, where exquisite Audrey Hepburn enjoys her breakfast (pastry and coffee) while gazing through the Tiffany's store window.

TOYOTA AND LEXUS

The Toyota Motor Company, a Japanese carmaker, was founded in 1937 by Kiichiro Toyoda and has since then become the largest automobile manufacturer in the world by sales, producing more than 7 million cars a year. It is located in Toyota City, Aichi Province, Japan. Mr. Akio Toyoda, a direct descendant of the company founder, has been CEO of Toyota Motor Corporation since 2009. The Toyota logo consists of two small ovals inscribed in a larger third oval, symbolising respectively the customer, the product, and the technological advances. There is a somewhat vague resemblance to a letter "T" (October 1989). The Toyota marketing is done by Saatchi & Saatchi in California. The famous

"Today. Tomorrow. Toyota" slogan was invented by them and was introduced in 2004–05.[†]

Toyota is famed for the reliability of its luxury Lexus brand (which later expanded into less luxurious cars), with its own logo (a capital L in italics – not very recognisable as an L – and inscribed in an oval; by Molly Designs and Hunter Communications) and its own slogan, **"the pursuit of perfection"** (by Tom Cordner, then at Saatchi & Saatchi; 1989[‡]), sometimes with the word **"relentless"** in front of "pursuit". A nice recent 1 minute 1 second ad promoting the Toyota-Lexus brand (Lexus LS 460) shows five successive scenes: the "pursuit of control" (prancing horse); the "pursuit of performance" (speed boat); the "pursuit of beauty" (alpinist); the "pursuit of exhilaration" (sky-diver); and the "pursuit of silence" (canoes on a lake). The ad finishes with the overall slogan written above. The piano music is by Mike Joggerst. The Lexus ad agency is Team One, a division of Saatchi & Saatchi, located in El Segundo, California and headed since 2008 by Jack Mickle.

VIRGIN ATLANTIC

A relatively young airline (maiden flight dating back to June 1984), Virgin Atlantic belongs 51% to Richard Branson's Virgin Group and 49% to Singapore Airlines. It operates both from Gatwick (initially its sole hub) and Heathrow.

The company has been extremely prolific slogan-wise. Some of these slogans have been aimed directly at competitors, such as **"No Way BA/AA"**, protesting in the late 1990s against the proposed British Airways/American Airlines partnership, which was finalised in February 1999.

The ad accompanying the excellent slogan **"Love at First Flight"**, which celebrated in 2009 the airline's 25th anniversary, shows a fleet of glamorous stewardesses in red arriving for the inaugural flight, while one onlooker says, "I need to change my ticket". The

† Thank you to Ms Claire Patel for this information.

‡ Thank you to Noppol Thongnop (Team One) for this information.

playful film was created by Tractor and produced by Tim Page for RKCR/Y&R. Yet the most intriguing recent slogans have been those introduced to promote Virgin Atlantic's "Upper Class": **"je ne sais quoi. defined"** and **"fear of not flying"**.

The first slogan, again by RKCR/Y&R, was meant to accompany still ads and was supposed to underline "the magic ingredient which sets Virgin apart from the competition". It daringly uses a French expression "*je ne sais quois*" meaning "something not easy to define", where possibly the addition of "defined" is somewhat contradictory. As for the second slogan, by Y&R New York, it attempts to go against the mainstream thinking insofar as the fear of flying is a real one for many people. The ad accompanying this slogan shows a woman saying, "There are only four things I'm afraid of: bees, spiders, wolves and being in a flight that doesn't have direct aisle access like Virgin Atlantic does . . ."

Last but not least, the daringly provocative 1 minute 30 second 2010 TV ad accompanying the slogan **"Your airline's got it . . ."**, again by RKCR/Y&R, shows some shots which may become memorable – such as the stewardess carrying an ice-cream tray and who melts away when passengers try to touch her. It finishes with the tagline (while a Virgin plane flies above), "Is that Linda?" "No, she's in Miami". The music, by Muse trio and inspired by Nina Simone's "Feeling Good", is just great.

VODAFONE

Vodafone, headquartered in Newbury, Berkshire, is the world's largest telecommunications company as measured by revenues, and the fourth largest company quoted on the FTSE 100 (London Stock Exchange). Quite young (founded in 1984), Vodafone is headed up (since 2008) by Italian businessman Vittorio Colao. The company has been criticised for agreeing to the Egyptian government's request to shut down its network during the early 2011 uprising. But it replies that its slogan **"Power to you"** (see below) was an important incentive for the Egyptian people.

Vodafone's logo is called the **"speechmark logo"** and consists of a red opening quotation mark on a white circular background. The quotation mark "suggests conversation" but I must say that, although I am a Vodafone customer, I failed to recognise the meaning of the red figure until I read up about the company. Over the last ten years Vodafone has had three successive slogans. The slogan **"How are you?"** was introduced in 2001. One October 2007 TV ad (1 minute) using this slogan shows a series of joyful events ("We're off . . . We're gorgeous . . . We're free . . . We're in love . . . We're safe . . . We're winning", with an interlude at the opera where a man called on his phone answers "I'm not here") enjoyed by Vodafone users. It finishes with a Vodafone banner together with "The people you need are only a touch away. **How are you?**". The second slogan, branded in 2005 by ad agencies JWT and BBH, is **"Make the most of now"**. It bears some resemblance to Microsoft's **"Where do we go today?"** but is affirmative rather than interrogative. The slogan **"Power to you"**, the most striking in my opinion, was introduced by Argentinian ad agency Santos in 2009. A moving 1 minute film (May 2010) shows a gentleman being honoured at a business dinner. His daughter phones him on his mobile: "Dad, he's left me." "Where are you?", he asks. Then he leaves the meeting and arrives hurriedly in a taxi. She falls into his arms: "You weren't doing anything, were you?" "No, just emptying the dishwasher", he replies. And Vodafone concludes with its slogan and the sentence "People depend on our network".

VOLVO

Just as Jaguar now belongs to an Indian company, Volvo now belongs (after a long period from 1999 to 2010 in the hands of Ford Motor Co) to a Chinese company, Zhejiang Geely Holding Group based in Hangzhou, Zhejiang, China. The holding group also owns an important Chinese automobile manufacturer with four brands (Emgrand, Englon, Gleagle and Geely). The company headquarters are still in Göteborg, Sweden. Volvo dates back to 14 April 1927, when the first Volvo ÖV 4 car was produced. The founders were Assar Gabrielsson and Gustav Larson. Volvo's reputation – and advertising – was long built on its reliability and, of course, on its capacity to withstand the cold weather of Scandinavia. However, this "sturdiness" became more and more a liability in Europe where customers preferred lighter, flashier albeit less sturdy cars. Volvo's ad agency, "team Volvo", presently consists of people from Havas and Euro RSCG. It is based in Amsterdam and, since 2010, led by Jorian Murray.

The famous **"For life"** slogan was introduced in 1999 by Swedish ad agency Forsman and Bodenfors (based in Göteborg; Staffan Forsman, Sven-Olof Bodenfors; Art Director Mikko Timonen; Copywriter Jones Enghage), and US agency Messner Vetere (based in New York; Thomas Messner and Barry Vetere) who have had the Volvo account since 1990–91. Volvo's recent TV ads now focus on the car's speed and braking capacity. In a film boasting the S60, with Astor Piazzolla's "Libertango" as background, you see a high-speed Volvo putting the brakes on to avoid a glass of water; the glass falls over only when the car turns around. Another recent video (30 seconds, January 2011) has the title "How to make a sexy car ad" and has four parts:

1)   "Show a sexy car" (shows the Volvo V60);

2)   "Include a visual metaphor" (shows the head of a black panther – a jaguar would have been a mistake!);

3)   "Make it all wet and steamy" (shows a wet Volvo under sleet and rain; at first very surprising but grows on you);

4)   "Finish with an obscure product demo" – the panther jumps into the trunk of the Volvo.

The excellent music is by Marius Rypdal. A third video goes as far as using tarot cards to vaunt the S60 R-Design. Volvo has recently introduced the slogan **"There's more to life than sexy cars"** (an apparent criticism of their own models), to which they have added – in lesser bold print – **"No, wait a second – there isn't"**.

THE WALL STREET JOURNAL (WSJ)

Famous in finance, the *Wall Street Journal* (WSJ) was founded on 8 July 1889 by Charles Dow, Edward Jones and Charles Bergstresser and published by their Dow Jones & Company. The statement of purpose was "to give fully and fairly the daily news attending the fluctuations in prices of stocks, bonds, and some classes of commodities. It will aim steadily at being a paper of news and not a paper of opinions". Dow and Jones went on to launch the famed "Dow Jones Average" on 26 May 1896 – at the beginning only 12 company stocks were concerned. After belonging to the family of journalist Clarence Barron from 1902 till 2007, the WSJ was purchased by news tycoon Rupert Murdoch. Although the journal has not been accused of any wrongdoing whatsoever, Lee Hinton, the top executive of Dow Jones & Co, resigned on 15 July 2011 in the midst of the news hacking scandal. The company announced that there would be no replacement for the time being. The worldwide circulation of WSJ is more than 2 million, while there are some 400,000 online paying subscribers, including yours truly.

In 1985 young ad agency Fallon McElliott (Minneapolis; now part of Publicis) launched the slogan **"The daily diary of the American dream"** for the journal. The repetition of the three "d" words is good but the word "American" is now superseded by the fact that the WSJ publishes both a European and an Asian edition. In January 2010, after an earlier attempt at **"Every journey needs a journal"** with a video starring trumpeter Wynton Marsalis (September 2010), a more far-reaching and general slogan, **"Live in the know"**, was launched by the McGarryBowen New York ad agency (Chief Creative Officer, Gordon Bowen), which now belongs to Dentsu. The slogan implies that by reading the WSJ, one gains better knowledge and thereby better living.

XBOX (MICROSOFT)

The Xbox 360 is one of Microsoft's spearheads and has been extremely successful, with more than 53 million copies sold as of spring 2011. It is in competition with other video game consoles, such as Sony's PS3, but, as one of my sons puts it, the Xbox 360 is "super nice". Microsoft's Chairman of the Board is Bill Gates and the CEO is Steve Ballmer; the company is located in Redmond, Washington State, USA. The Xbox 360 was launched in October/

November 2005 in different versions ("Core" or "Arcadia" – lower range; "Pro" or "Premium" – middle-range; "Elite" – top range, slightly later). In June 2010 an Xbox 360 S series with more storage space was launched. The Xbox 360 logo is a silver sphere cut in four by a parallel and a meridian of greenish-yellow colour. In TV ads, there is an additional swirl.

In November 2005, Microsoft accompanied the new Xbox 360 with the slogan **"Jump in"** (McCann Erickson San Francisco, Creative Directors Scott Duchon and Geoff Edwards)[†]. In a 30-second TV ad "Live your Moment" (September 2008) one sees a young lady smiling mysteriously; she's joined by a boyfriend, and when she turns around you see the back of her skull open to show the two looking at a movie! The tagline is "Download movies on Xbox 360!" (this has indeed been possible since November 2006). Since the introduction of the 360 S series in June 2010, you can even use the Xbox, thanks to a special "Kinect" sensor device, to move – for instance dance – *at a distance* from the Xbox. In an autumn 2010 1 minute 2 second ad, a man sitting on a sofa with his girlfriend announces: "Xbox Play!" You see the pair and others dancing and moving in front of their Xbox, somewhat like in a gym. An off-screen voice says: "You don't need to know anything you don't already know or do anything you don't already do. All you have to do is be you. **You** are the controller . . . Introducing Kinect for Xbox 360."

XEROX

Xerox Corp is one of those rare success stories where a superb scientific discovery leads to a worldwide corporation. The company was founded in 1906 in Rochester, NY, as the Haloid Photographic Company by Joseph C. Wilson, then transferred to his son, and later, to grandson Joseph C. Wilson (1909–71). The present CEO is Ursula M. Burns, and the headquarters are located in Norwalk, connecticut. I still vividly remember the 1960–1 day when several Harvard chemistry colleagues invited me to see the

---

† Thank you to Mary Best Barney for this information.

new Xerox 914 machine which could make seven paper copies in a minute via a complex electrostatic method – we were flabbergasted! I also remember the craze which shortly followed the introduction in July 1961 of Xerox on the New York Stock Exchange. The stock price multiplied by nearly 10 in a single summer!

The first slogan for Xerox was **"The Document Company"**, as of August 1994, with the assistance of Landor Associates advertising company (then Managing Director was Peter J. Harleman).[†] At the same time the logo – which had been a blue Xerox on a white background – switched to a **red** Xerox below the slogan in black (see www.instantshift.com/2009/01/29/20-corporate-brand-logo-evolution/). On 7 September 2010 the company introduced the slogan **"Ready for real business"**, which was accompanied by several TV ads (ad agency Young & Rubicam, New York; Executive Creative Directors Ian Reichenthal and Scott Vitrone; global media agency MEC, New York; digital marketing agency VML, Kansas City). In one 33-second commercial in September 2010, "Mr. Met" (baseball head; 00 number on his back) meets two Xerox executives who ask him whether he's finished his sales brochure for the club. They first criticise his proposal, but then say "I love it. I love it, it's great". The tagline: "The Mets know it's better for Xerox to design and produce their direct mail, so they can focus on entertaining their fans".

† Thank you to Robert Corbishley, European PR Manager at Xerox, for this information.

PART 3
INDEXES

COMPANY NAME AND BRAND INDEX

THEMATIC INDEX

NOTE: Numbers in brackets refer to slogan number.

30811539R00141

Made in the USA
Lexington, KY
17 March 2014